RESIDENTIAL REMODELING AND RENOVATION

Completing the Exterior and Interior of Your Home

FREDERICK UHLEN HOP

PRENTICE HALL, Englewood Cliffs, New Jersey 07632

Library of Congress Cataloging-in-Publication Data

Hop, Frederick Uhlen, (date).
    Residential remodeling and renovation.

    Includes index.
    1. Dwellings—Remodeling. I. Title.
TH4816.H655 1988   643'.7   87-17527
ISBN 0-13-775255-5

Editorial/production supervision and
    interior design: *Carol L. Atkins*
Cover design: *Photo Plus Art*
Manufacturing buyer: *Peter Havens*

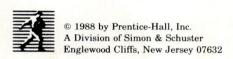

© 1988 by Prentice-Hall, Inc.
A Division of Simon & Schuster
Englewood Cliffs, New Jersey 07632

Printed in the United States of America

10 9 8 7 6 5 4 3 2 1

ISBN 0-13-775255-5

Prentice-Hall International (UK) Limited, *London*
Prentice-Hall of Australia Pty. Limited, *Sydney*
Prentice-Hall Canada, Inc., *Toronto*
Prentice-Hall Hispanoamericana, S.A., *Mexico*
Prentice-Hall of India Private Limited, *New Delhi*
Prentice-Hall of Japan, Inc., *Tokyo*
Simon & Schuster Asia Pte. Ltd., Singapore
Editora Prentice-Hall do Brasil, Ltda., *Rio de Janeiro*

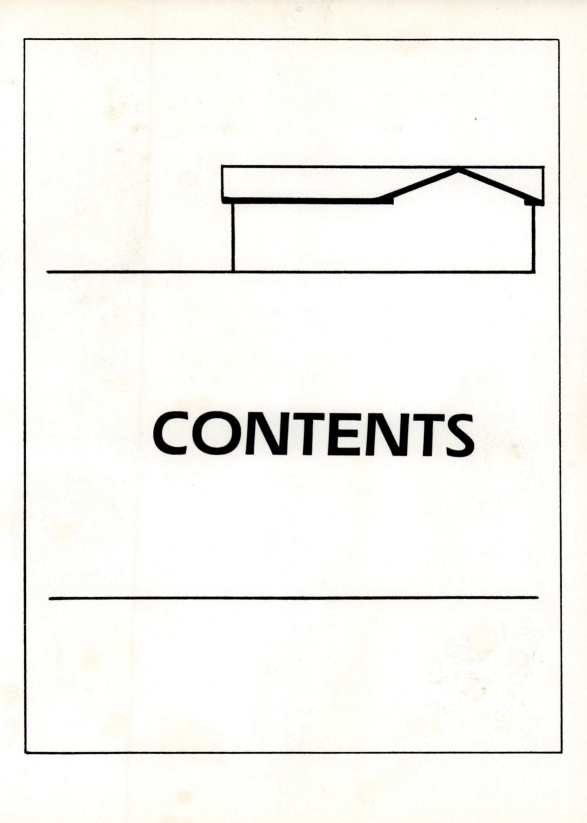

CONTENTS

PART 2
INTERIOR COMPLETION

5 PRINCIPLES OF UTILITY INSTALLATION   61

6 CABINET SOFFITS   85

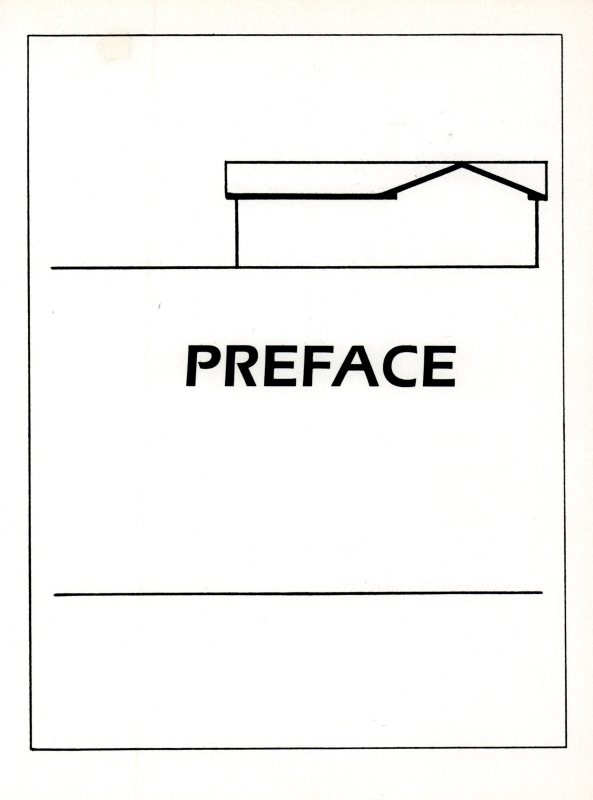

PREFACE

The finishing phase of home building begins as soon as the structural components have been assembled, erected, and covered with a protective roof. Now the aesthetics, the features that beautify and individualize the home, are ready to be put on display.

Up until now there may have been a little hedging with the rough construction. "If it is strong enough, it will be all right since all will be covered up later," is sometimes the theme. Now every detail, every feature, will be on display. Can we do it? Can we really pull it off? This book will tell you how to go about the projects and in what order. By accumulating the know-how you will be encouraged to try phase two, the actual doing.

Part 1 covers those items on the exterior of the house that usually come first. Window, door, and siding installation are covered in primer style. Tried and proven techniques are explained and illustrated.

Part 2 leads us indoors, where we start at the beginning and work our way through the miracle of turning a studded shell into a home of beauty and grace.

This book will especially help the shell buyer who commits to completing and finishing a framed-only structure. Those embarking on a remodeling or renovation project will find the book valuable. Even the person who has a singular project interest at the moment, such as paneling or hanging a door, will find the resources here and may be encouraged to go on to greater projects.

It is my hope that those with minimum experience and tentative confidence will be encouraged to go forward with their dreams and that the old pros who read this book will smile with the recognition of techniques that work—and possibly find a new idea or two as well.

Frederick Uhlen Hop

PART 1

EXTERIOR COMPLETION

1 CLOSING IN THE HOUSE

In the sequence of building a structure where wood is the primary material, the weather will play an important role. Rain, snow, and ice can play havoc with building materials. Therefore, a primary objective is to close in the house as quickly as possible. The first goal of closing in is to roof the structure so that no rain will enter via the top. The second goal is to install windows and doors for further protection of the interior of the house. Most roof and floor deck sheathing materials in use today are laminates and wafer types held together with waterproof glue. The glue is of high quality and impervious to water, but the wood itself will soak up moisture, permitting its fibers to separate. Such separation takes place readily where knotholes are present on a surface layer of plywood sheathing. Edges where end grain is exposed are particularly vulnerable. These types of fabricated sheathing are not intended to resist or withstand repeated soakings over extended periods of exposure. Once the roofing is completed and the windows and doors (temporary or permanent) have been installed, the structure is said to be closed in.

Many builders prefer to hang a temporary door on the entrance through which materials will continue to be carried. There is much to be said in favor of this technique, as it will usually avoid damage to the permanent door jamb and casement. An old door from a salvage yard or a cut-down piece of plywood will serve. Where the door will be carried from job to job, surface hinges may be screwed to the door and nailed to the rough opening with duplex form nails.

2 WINDOW INSTALLATION

Several window casement designs on the market require particular installation techniques. Regardless of any uniqueness, common objectives exist. The unit should be hung plumb, level, and square. If it is an opening-type sash, it should open and close flawlessly. It should be supported under the lower corners. It should not depend solely on nails through its flanges for support.

Windows with integral jambs and sills are placed in the opening from the outside, as are flange types. The frame is first centered in the opening at the bottom. A level is placed on the windowsill (not on the sash). This is one of the few places in a house where a 24 or 28″ level is used effectively. Place shims under a vertical jamb that checks low until the windowsill checks level. Place shims above the ends of the jambs under the header. The sill and the headboard should now check level. Place the level against the vertical jamb on one side. Move the frame to the right or left at the top until the jamb checks plumb. Check the other jamb. It should check plumb also. If it does not check plumb, measure the distance between the jambs at the bottom and top. If the distances are not identical, the frame is not a perfect rectangle. In this case, compromise by moving the top of the frame in a direction that will cause the level to read the same amount in or out of plumb on each side. In other words, this imperfect window rectangle will be plumb on its vertical center line.

If the top and bottom widths are nearly perfect but the frame will not check plumb on both sides, it is likely that one or both sides are bowed. Hold a straight-edged board of a length close to the window height against the frame. Locate the bow. If the frame is bowed toward the rough-opening trimmer, you are in luck. Simply shim between the jamb and trimmer until it checks straight and plumb (Fig. 1-1). It will be necessary to place shims at the edge of the top and bottom of the frame on the opposite side to prevent the whole frame from moving over.

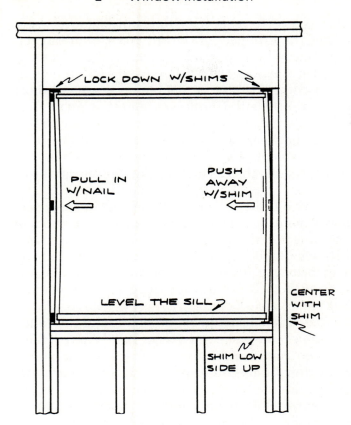

LOCK DOWN W/SHIMS

PULL IN
W/NAIL

PUSH
AWAY
W/SHIM

LEVEL THE SILL

CENTER
WITH
SHIM

SHIM LOW
SIDE UP

Figure 1-1 Place shims to hold jambs straight whether bowed in or bowed out.

If the frame bows in toward the sash, a more difficult problem is faced. Ultimately, that frame will have to be held straight permanently with shims and a nail or two through the jamb. It is better to do the alignment with a clamp temporarily than with a nail. In any case, the distance across the vertical jambs cannot be less than it is at the top or bottom because the sash will not operate properly.

If it is not possible to plumb the vertical jambs because one of them ends up against the top face of the wall trimmer before it is plumb, the bottom of the frame will need to be moved away from that side of the opening. The best possible position of the frame will be attained when the opposite corners from top to bottom are equally spaced away from the trimmers (upper right and lower left, upper left and lower right).

A final check is made in two ways. Use a framing square in the lower corners of the jamb. Each corner should check square.

Any variation will be cause to reset the shims until squareness is attained. Do not alter the levelness of the sill after its initial setting. When satisfied that all is square and plumb and the frame is solidly held by shims, operate the sash to see if it functions smoothly without binding. Under a double-hung sash, there should be no crack above the sill. Check a casement window from the outside. A casement window swings out on vertical hinges like a door. The clearance between the window frame and the jamb should be parallel on all sides. Any variation is cause to reset the casing. Perfect installation is the essence of trouble-free operation in years to come.

Fastening the casing (the exterior trim) or the flange is next in order. Wooden casement trim is called brickmold. It is prudent to predrill this molding for the nails to prevent splitting. Only rust-resistant nails should be used. Hot-dipped galvanized are best. The length will depend on the type of backing behind the mold. Soft sheathing such as Styrofoam or blackboard does not provide adequate backing.

A 1 × 2 surround of wood should be nailed around the rough opening before the frame wall is sheathed (Fig. 1-2). Where a table saw is available, this surround material can be ripped from precut stud lumber or any scrap dimension lumber (1½″ thick) most economically.

A seal (2 to 4″ strip of 15-pound building paper) is stapled over the surround and sheathing. Start at the bottom. Lap the side strips over the top edge of the bottom strips. Lap the top strip over the top ends of the side strips. These strips help protect against infiltration of unwanted air.

Where wooden surrounds are used, a 10d hot-dipped galvanized cup head or casing nail will be adequate to hold brickmolding. Over blackboard (no surrounds) a 16d hot-dipped casing nail will probably be required in order to get adequate penetration into the wood behind the sheathing. Place a nail within 2 to 3″ from each corner. Space the other nails about 10 to 12″ apart. Each nail will be close to the outer edge of the brickmold and slanted toward the trimmer stud behind. Predrilled holes will prevent splitting. Cup heads and casing heads are not large. Keep the tap hole diameter smaller than the nail shank so that the heads will have adequate holding capacity.

The flanged window has a little less leeway for nailing. The

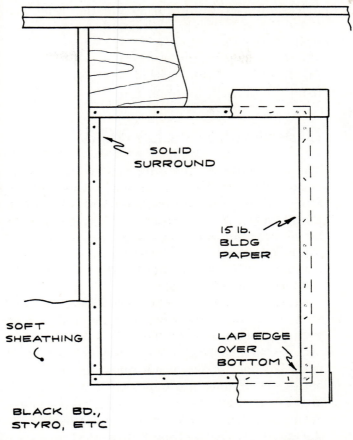

Figure 1-2 With soft-type sheathings, a solid wood surround of the same thickness is nailed around the opening and then covered with a 4″ strip of building paper.

rough-in size listed for this window style is often larger than neces-sary if a building is quite plumb. The flanges are of minimum width to cover such a wide gap between the window jamb and the trimmer. With excellent plumbness, there is adequate flange to reach onto the surround. An opening that is not quite plumb may result in a flange whose edge just barely reaches onto the sur-rounding surface. To accommodate this minimum coverage at cer-tain points on the flange, holes must be drilled close to the edges of the flange. Big-headed nails are best. A 1½″ galvanized roofing nail slanted toward the solid wood will be a good choice. Unlike the brickmold, an aluminum or plastic flange should be drilled with holes larger than the nail shank so that there is no bind and the nail can be slanted adequately. When nailing the flange, a guard should be held between the nail and the jamb. A piece of sheet metal or thin Masonite or plywood will protect the edge of the jamb from a wayward hammer blow.

3 DOOR INSTALLATION

The technique of "hanging" a door has undergone several modifications since the coming of hollow-core prehung doors. As little as four decades ago, the method was to install a wooden jamb as plumb and square as possible. Then the door was fitted to the jamb by planing off the edges and ends. This traditional installation method seldom netted a perfectly square door. The hinges were morticed (chiseled in flush) with hand tools. Some of the older installations had morticed jambs for the hinge butt with a surface-mounted hinge leaf on the door. This was called a face butt or half-butt. These old hinges are valuable antiques now. They coordinate with porcelain door knobs.

Today's carpenter will usually hang the jamb and door as a unit. The door serves as a large squaring device, which facilitates a better job. Hinges are morticed into the jamb and door before the unit is installed. Hinge-morticing jigs make it possible to rout a perfectly aligned door-to-jamb relationship. A power router does the cutting. Lacking this professional setup, a skilled amateur can still do an adequate job with hammer and chisel and the proper information.

HINGE POSITION

A primary visual indicator that exposes amateur or nonconformist construction technique is to see hinges on doors that are not positioned according to the industry standard. The Stanley Builders Kit probably did more to standardize hinge location on passage doors than any other factor in the history of construction. This placement jig has several options intended for different hinge quantities and sizes.

THE SEVEN-ELEVEN RULE

When two hinges are used on a lightweight door, or as an economy measure, the "seven-eleven" rule is used. This means that the upper edge of the top hinge will be 7″ down from the door top. The lower edge of the bottom hinge is 11″ above the door bottom.

The "five and ten" rule is used for doors with three hinges. Three hinges are required on a heavy door such as a solid framed panel door or a solid slab door. Some good-quality homes where economy is not an objective will have three hinges on all passage doors. The five and ten formula places the top hinge down 5″, the lower hinge up 10″ from the bottom, and a third hinge centered between the two.

Whether the hinges are set with a jig or by measurement the seven-eleven and the five and ten rule should be adhered to routinely; otherwise, the builder's knowledge is suspect and may give cause to doubt other more significant features of the construction.

Positioning the hinge butt across the edge of the door relates to the casement thickness that will project beyond the jamb (beyond the door and wall surface). The pivot point of the hinge pin determines how far out the door surface will be swung. The door must clear the casement trim; otherwise, the hinges will be torn loose. The Stanley jig and other jig brands control this location of the hinge butt automatically. A distance of 1⅛″ across the door edge will be adequate to clear casement moldings up to ⅝″. For thicker moldings, keep in mind that the vertical center line of the hinge pin must be beyond the surface of the door at least as much as the thickness of the casement trim; otherwise, the trim board will present a fulcrum to the door surface when the door is opened to its extremity and the hinge screws will be torn out.

Morticing the door and jamb requires craftsmanship and precision. Any misalignment, no matter how small, will cause stress on the screws. Eventually, the screws will pull loose, having stripped out their anchor holes. Perfect alignment exists when the pins of all the hinges are on a common axis, a center line that runs vertically through the center of them all.

Perfect alignment is achieved by understanding and accepting certain principles and by adopting a perfectionist state of mind. These are the principles:

- Each hinge must be parallel with both the door edges and the jamb edges.
- The setback of each hinge butt must be identical to all others on both the door and the jamb.
- Corresponding distances between the hinges must be identical on the door and jamb.
- The mortices on the door edge must be a minimum of $1/8''$ higher than on the jamb to provide clearance above the door when closed.

The last principle deserves comment. The Stanley jig has a little metal flipper on the end. Its purpose is to gauge this clearance. The flipper is turned down to hook over the door top. On the jamb, its outer surface is aligned flush with the lower edge of the top jamb dado. The metal flipper gauge is about $1/16''$ thick. This is not enough clearance between the door and the jamb. Two or three coats of varnish on each surface will close the clearance gap considerably. The slightest swelling of the wood from moisture in the house is apt to cause a sticking door. A $1/8''$ minimum space will usually prove more trouble-free from the outset.

   This is a good place to caution against omitting the finishing (sealing the wood) of the top and bottom of doors. A most important element in the prevention of door swelling is to make certain that all wood surfaces are well sealed. The most vulnerable part of wood is the open end grain. On a door, this is found on the top and bottom at the corners where the vertical door frame ends are exposed. Any door, whether or not trimmed at the top or bottom, should be sealed. Because these surfaces are not seen they are frequently left unfinished. These unseen surfaces do not necessarily require cosmetic stain; nonetheless, they should be sealed with varnish together with the rest of the door.

SETTING A DOOR LOCK

Door locksets are referred to as entrance, passage, or closet types. An entrance set is the locking type furnished with two keys. Locksets can usually be purchased in quantities with common keys. This is a convenience where several exterior entrances exist. One key will open all doors. It also provides additional keys at the outset so that duplicates do not have to be made for various members of the family.

Passage door sets are available with or without locks. The locking type is tripped from one side only and is referred to as a privacy lock. This type is customarily installed on bathroom doors and sometimes on adult bedroom doors. All other passage doors will have a simple latching function.

A closet door may be secured with a regular passage set that includes a knob on both sides, a bolt, and a strike plate. A simplified closet latch set is one that includes only a dummy knob. Spring catches or magnetic catches are used to hold the door shut in the same manner as a cabinet door.

Installation of a lockset (Fig. 1-3) is covered by an instruction sheet furnished by the manufacturer. Although a person may have installed many locksets before, it will be wise to glance over the instruction sheet when a different brand is encountered. The specifications may vary.

Placement of the lockset is important. There will be a template in the box, which is to be folded around the edge of the door. There are prick points to establish the hole centers for the bolt and the shaft. The height of the set location is not usually specified. As for hinges, there is a standard location for the lockset that should be followed. It is 36″ above the bottom of the door.

Beveling the door edge will usually be required where no more than ⅛″ of clearance exists. A tightly fitted door may have clearance in the closed position but will fail to clear while being shut. This is because the diagonal distance from the hinge pivot

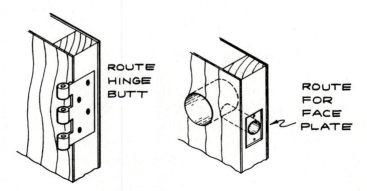

ROUTE HINGE BUTT

ROUTE FOR FACE PLATE

Figure 1-3 Standard door hinge and latch borings.

point to the back edge of the latch edge is greater than the face width of the door. To overcome this clearance problem, a bevel is planed on the lockset edge. The bevel need only be enough so that clearance exists for the edge to clear the jamb. Too much bevel will cause an alignment problem where the bolt plate seats in the door edge. Regardless of how much bevel exists, the bolt plate will still remain square with the door face. Therefore, a slight misalignment in parallelism will exist between the bolt plate and the door edge. The bolt runs into the door parallel to the door faces and on a center line with the door thickness. Therefore, the bolt face will be square, at right angles, to the door faces. The bolt face cannot be angled to fit flush with a beveled edge. In order for no edge of the bolt face to protrude above the wood surface, the edge on the low side of the bevel will be morticed deep enough for the plate edge to be flush. On the high side of the bevel, the plate will be slightly below the surface. The bolt face mortice should be made before beveling the door when using a power router. The router can then bear on the full surface of the square edge. The mortice will need to be deep enough to take into consideration the amount of wood that will be removed by beveling the edge.

In order not to alter the doorknob distance from the edge, one must adapt by moving the knob shaft hole farther from the door edge an amount equal to the bevel. Where the bevel is slight ($\frac{1}{16}''$ or less) the adaptation is made by placing the punch prick template on the back side of the door after it has been beveled.

Where one is willing to accept a wider crack between the door edge and the jamb (about $\frac{3}{16}$ to $\frac{1}{4}''$), no beveling is required. The marking template can be used on either face of the door, and the bolt face will be flush all around its four edges.

HANGING THE JAMB

The door jamb is hung in basically the same manner as a window casement. It is centered, squared, plumbed, shimmed, and nailed through the jambs. Unlike the usual window, a door receives a horizontal shock each time it is shut forcibly (slammed). The vertical door jambs require adequate anchoring to the trimmers to withstand this direction of force. Nails of adequate length and diameter are driven through the jambs and directly under or through the shims. Plywood shims will split the least. Three mil and $\frac{1}{4}''$ panel scraps are good. Where two or more pieces of wood are used to build up an adequate thickness, a little glue between each will prevent them from falling away when split by a nail.

Nails to use may include cuphead finish nails or casing nails of a 6d to 8d size. Box nails, with their larger heads, are most effective, but should only be used where the door stop will cover them. Since the shims are frequently placed directly behind the hinge mortices, they provide an index for locating three of the nails on the hinge jamb. No more nails are used between the hinges unless backed by shims because a nail in an unbacked location will pull the jamb out of line. Where the holding power of the trimmer is inferior due to the softness of the wood, the builder will opt for a minimum of six nails placed one directly above and one below the hinge mortice locations and four nails equally spaced between.

Exterior doors require clearance at the bottom for a sealing sill. This type of threshold has a replaceable rubber or vinyl insert. The simplest type mounts on top of a wood threshold sill. Another style is wider and may incorporate a weather seal that is adjustable up and down under the door. A prehung steel door usually has this type. The prefabricated aluminum threshold is available in several heights. This is helpful where the framed opening is excessive in height. A taller threshold can provide a solution.

Trimming styles for exterior doors (Fig. 1-4) vary according to the architectural design of the house. Where patterned casing, such as brickmold, is used, the top corners will be mitered. The bottoms will have a square-cut receding bevel that matches the downward and outward slant of the threshold sill. The rain-shedding principle should be practiced with all exterior materials, including trimming boards. Any horizontal surfaces that are exposed to rain will deteriorate at an accelerated rate. Window and door sills are particularly vulnerable.

Board-and-batten rough-sawn-sided houses will likely have a simple 1 × 4 casing surround of the same material as the siding. Frequently, the headboard will extend out over the sideboards at the top corners. The sideboards will butt under the headboard with a square-cut end. The top end of these sideboards should be beveled about 5 to 10° and installed in a drain posture. The top board is beveled to match on both upper and lower edges. This is accomplished expediently where a jointer is on hand. It is no great task with a hand plane and soft wood such as rough-sawn cedar. The bevel on the top ends of the sideboards is matched to mate under

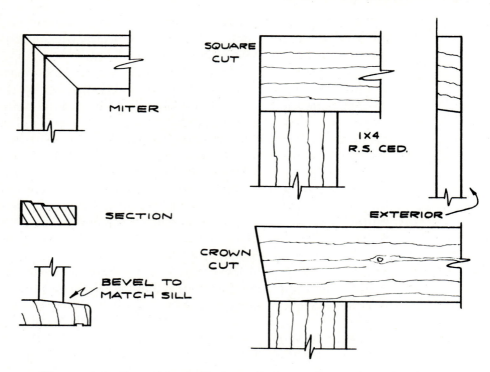

Figure 1-4 Contemporary door and window casing is mitered at the top corners and beveled at the bottom on the sill. Rough-sawn cedar trim is usually square cut or crown beveled at the head.

the edge bevel on the headboard. For this job of mating, a T bevel is a handy tool to have for checking the bevels. The 2 to 4″ strips of black building paper are stapled around the door jamb the same as on the window openings to seal against infiltration.

Nailing any kind of trim around a wood door jamb is a particular task at best. Some of the nails will be close to the inner edges of the casing. These must be slanted to enter the jamb. The surface contact area on the jamb is small. The casing is sometimes set back ½″ to form a rabbet, a door stop for a wood screen door. Metal combination storm and screen doors will not require so much drop-back, as they are surface mounted through flanges.

Nails along the outer edges of the casing are slanted toward the trimmer stud. There should be two nails, one on each edge, within 2 to 3″ of each end of each casing board. Do not place them directly opposite each other. Space all other nails about 12 to 16″ apart on each side. Stagger them a little from side to side. For example, after the two top and bottom nails, the next nail will be placed on the outer edge at the midpoint of the height. The remaining space above and below will contain two more nails each on third points. On a brickmold-style casing, this will average out to nails just under 12″ apart. The nails on the inner edge may be staggered down from the top miter cut so that each will be about 2″ lower than the outer nail position.

Lock the mitered corner joints at the top as soon as a couple of set nails have been placed in each of the three casing boards (Fig. 1-5). A small finishing nail (5, 6, or 7d) is driven down through the top of the headboard into the end of the side board miter. Off-center this nail a little. Drive another nail through the edge of the side board into the top board miter. Off-center this nail in the opposite direction so that it does not contact the top nail. These nails will assist the corner joint to maintain its surface alignment while the remainder of the fastening takes place.

Plumbing, leveling, and squaring a door jamb are more critical than for a window. A window can tilt in or out at the top in conjunction with an unplumb wall and have little effect on its functioning as long as its surface is on a straight plane. A door, by

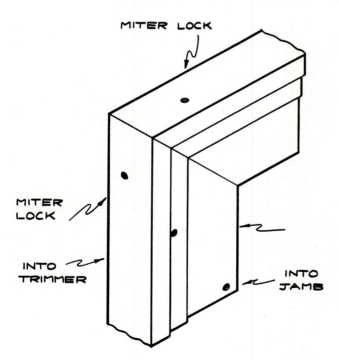

MITER LOCK

MITER
LOCK

INTO
TRIMMER

INTO
JAMB

Figure 1-5 Brickmold casing is locked at mitered corner with a vertical and a horizontal staggered nail.

comparison, will swing one way or another (toward closed or open) if the hinged side is not vertical both in the direction of the wall and at right angles to the wall. It is irritating to a homeowner to have to use a door stop to keep a door open.

Adjusting for verticality in an unplumb rough opening is difficult (where the top of the wall tilts in or out). One cannot set a jamb very far from parallel with the wall without causing major alignment problems with interior and exterior wall coverings. A wall frame that is more than ⅛″ out of plumb from interior to exterior should be rectified, at least at the door openings, before proceeding to install a door jamb.

The side jambs must be parallel vertically as well as plumb. It would seem to be obvious that if both jambs were plumb they would also be parallel. Here the element of human frailty enters the picture. A 4 or 6′ level is the standard tool for plumbing the edge of the jambs. The eye must center the bubble between the two lines precisely the same every time the level is used. It is impossible to be that perfect and consistent given the nature of the instrument. A final check should be made every time by standing a little way off and sighting across the edges of the jambs to ascertain their parallelism. This is often difficult or impossible where the door is in a confined area. Also, the distance between the jambs can be checked for uniformity at vertical intervals of about 12″.

Door sill installation method has undergone some transition over the years. The remodeler will find many old homes where an oak threshold was cut down into the floor header and joists. These members were chiseled out to accept the sill in a position that mated the top of the sill with the top of an oak or maple floor. Most modern door frame installations will have the sill resting on top of the subfloor. The underlayment floor layer butts the edge of the sill. A certain amount of the sill will protrude above the underlayment. This space is filled with carpet pad and carpet or ceramic tile. The threshold sealer provides enough more height to permit the door bottom to clear the carpeting.

The sequence of door jamb installation is the same as that of a window.

1. Center the sill and shim the lower corners of the jambs.
2. Plumb the side jambs.
3. Shim the side jambs at the top.

4. Shim between the header and the jamb tops.
5. Shim behind each hinge location. Make sure that the jamb is straight (not bowed toward or away from the opening).
6. Shim behind the striker plate.
7. Nail the jambs.
8. Nail the brickmold to the wall.

BOWED JAMBS

Jambs that insist on bowing into or away from the door opening will have to be held in position with additional shims and a well-placed nail (Fig. 1-6). If the jamb needs to be bent toward the opening, a finish nail may be used to hold the jamb and the shims in

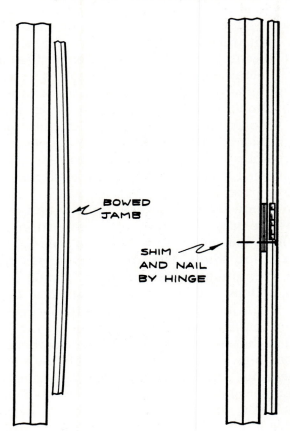

Figure 1-6 A shim maintains the desired distance between the jamb and the door trimmer. A headed nail holds the bowed jamb in against the trimmer stud.

place. Where the jamb has to be pulled toward the trimmer stud, a nail with a head is needed. Hot-dipped galvanized nails of 8d or 10d size or annular ringed flooring nails will be a good choice for the latter condition. Holding power is the basic requirement. Sink the nail head slightly below the surface with a ¼″ metal drift punch. Putty over the head before painting. The objective at completion of the installation is to have a door with a parallel clearance on the sides and top, a surface that is uniformly flush with the jambs all around, and a sill that seals tightly against infiltration. Obviously, the door should open and close flawlessly without great effort, and it should stand still in any position.

□ STORM DOOR INSTALLATION

There are three types of doors from which to choose that are hung on the outside of the exterior door jamb. The simple wood-framed screen door is in limited demand. Its days were numbered when the emphasis on fuel conservation became universal. The old-style screen door is still obtainable, however, and comes in standard door sizes. The full-picture-window glass door takes care of cold season needs. It is also prevalent in areas where utility use cycles from heat to air conditioning with minimum calendar days between. The combination door is the most adaptable door in use. This design incorporates both a screen and storm sash so that it can readily be changed from a closed winter mode to a warm-weather ventilating position.

Installing a wood-framed screen door is quite simple. Where butt hinges are used, the hinge butts are morticed into the screen door edge first. The door is then held in place in the casing with temporary spacing shims. The first attempt may reveal a need for planing. A minimum clearance of ⅛″ should be maintained on the top, bottom, and latch side after the door is permanently attached. When indexing the hinge butt mortices to the jamb, keep in mind that the hinge leaf thickness has not yet been inletted. It will add that much thickness to the clearance on the latch side after the hinge butts have been seated in their mortices.

Marking the hinge leaf locations on the jamb is most accurately done with a sharp thin-bladed knife. Press a slit into the jamb corner right at the edges of each hinge. A very sharp, hard lead pencil will also suffice. The old-style wood drafting pencil in a

lead grade from 5H to 9H makes an excellent marker for precision work.

Two other forms of hinges are available for wood screen doors. One is a half-surface-mount type. The surface-mount leaf is screwed on the face of the door, and the concealed leaf is morticed into the jamb. With this hinge type, the order of installing is reversed. The hinges are morticed and screwed to the jamb first. The door is then blocked in place and the surface-mount hinge leaves are screwed to the surface.

Another hinge type is the full surface mount. These can be obtained with or without integral door-closing springs. The full-surface-mount hinge is used only on flat casing. It is considered esthetically offensive to inlet a surface leaf into the contoured surface of brickmolding, thereby destroying the flow lines.

Full glass and combination storm doors on the modern market are made of aluminum or steel. They come complete with a flanged jamb. The entire unit is surface mounted with screws through predrilled holes. The flanges will mount on either brickmold or flat casing. Hang the unit with the door closed, being sure to maintain a parallel clearance at the top and latch side.

4 SIDING

The trim and siding phase comes next. Following the closing in of the openings, it becomes next in importance to cover the wall-sheathing materials against the deteriorating effects of sun and rain and against the potential of construction abuse. House frames sheathed with blackboard, and particularly Styrofoam, sheets are especially vulnerable to falling ladders, punctures from scaffold planks, and so on.

At this stage (closed in), some flexibility exists for priority setting and dealing with external influences. For example, on inclement days one can work on the interior provided that there are materials there awaiting installation. On good days, work may go forward wherever one chooses. A little preplanning will make the working conditions more enjoyable. For example, when installing siding during hot weather, it is often possible to work on the house side that is shaded and simply move around the house as the sun moves. In cold months, one can reverse the technique and manage to stay in the warming rays of the sun, except on the north side.

There is a practical consideration to this technique also. Bricks or stone should not be laid in the direct rays of the sun on hot days if it can be avoided (it usually can). Such a practice will cause the moisture to be quickly baked out of the mortar and the bricks. Adhesion is poor and the mortar will be weaker than if it had cured slowly.

☐ TYPES OF SIDING

There are many types of siding of various shapes and materials. Wood and stone were the original natural materials. People have fabricated many different types of materials since the days of laying one stone on another or one log on another.

Structural categories of most residences are called *masonry* or *wood-framed*. A masonry residence uses masonry products for both structural and veneer covering. In this classification, there are houses built of concrete blocks and those of double-walled brick (solid or cavity type). The wood-framed category includes houses that appear to be brick masonry but which are in reality brick veneered. Brick veneer or masonry veneer includes those structures that are framed and basically built of wood. The veneer is merely a covering that bears none of the weight of the structure. The brick or stone is then classified as a siding. Most homes being built today with brick and stone facing are of the veneer design because of the superior capacity for insulating the cavity and face of the frame wall. Conversely, most large apartment houses and commercial buildings are masonry and steel because of superiority in fire protection and permanency.

Wood siding can be had in a variety of types, shapes, and sizes (Fig. 1-7). The intent of this text is not encyclopedic; therefore, the concentration will be on installation techniques for common types and on significant pitfalls.

CLAPBOARD

Clapboard (bevel siding) has been around for a long time. In its original form, the homebuilder simply lapped the lower edge of one board over the top edge of the board below, thereby creating a water-shedding effect. The design ultimately developed into a

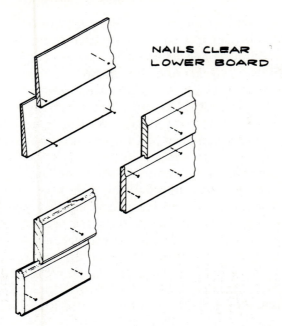

NAILS CLEAR
LOWER BOARD

Figure 1-7 Three types of traditional siding.

cross-section shape that tapered from a thick bottom to a thin top edge. Two rules are worthy of memorization and practice.

- Nail into solid backing (wood).
- Nail only through the outer layer of siding (just above the board below).

Few houses under construction today will be completely sheathed in wood. Some will have a sheet of plywood on each side of a corner to function as a wind brace. Most house frames will be covered with soft insulating materials such as fiberboard (blackboard) or Styrofoam. These types of sheathing do not anchor nails. Therefore, it is imperative that the nail location on horizontal siding types be directly over a stud and that the nail be long enough to penetrate the stud adequately to ensure holding the siding on. The amount of penetration needed is dependent on the stud hardness. Red fir and southern yellow pine, for example, will hold a nail with 1″ penetration, whereas spruce will need 1½″ or more.

The nail position, or distance up from the bottom edge, is determined by the amount of lap. Nails are placed only along the lower edge of each board. The nail must *not* go through the top edge of the board being lapped (Fig. 1-8). After installation, the siding will shrink a little. If a board is pinned on both lower and upper edges, the shrinkage will cause it to crack horizontally down a grain line. A secondary reason for not double-pinning horizontal siding is replacement ease. Should a board anywhere up the wall be damaged by a falling limb, a car bumper, or whatever, it can be slipped out and replaced without disturbing the remainder of the siding. The nails should be placed just far enough up from the edge to clear the top of the board underneath.

Hardboard siding comes in sheet form for vertical application and planks for horizontal application. The latter are 12″ wide by 16′ long. This Masonite-type material is usually primed on at least the edges and face, and some brands are primed on all surfaces. A bundle will usually contain a manufacturer's instruction sheet. These instructions should be followed for two reasons. The manufacturer has usually field tested the material to determine a satisfactory method. Second, when the instructions are not followed, there is little ground for complaint or adjustment should the system fail. Basically, hardboard manufacturers recommend the same nailing technique as that described previously for use with wood lap siding. Some recommend nailing through the upper lapped edge of the board below.

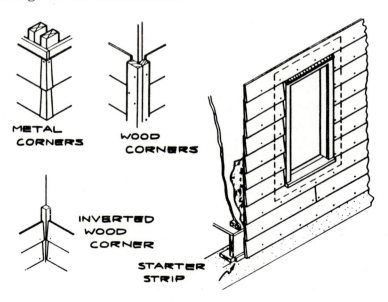

Figure 1-8 Details for installing bevel siding.

Starter strips for beveled or lapped horizontal siding are needed under the first course. Without this spacer the bottom boards would lie flat against the sheathing. The face would not be on the same angle as the boards above, which are lapped. The starter strip should be the same thickness as the part lapped above. Stock material can be purchased for starter strips, but it is costly. All forms available are sold by the linear foot at premium rates. The least costly alternative is to rip strips to the correct thickness from economy, precut stud material. Hardboard siding planks are not beveled. They are of uniform thickness throughout. Once a job is underway, or if this type of siding has been used on a previous house, scraps will be available. Strips can be ripped from the scraps. Make the strips the same width as the amount of lap.

FRIEZE BOARD

A frieze is a decorative board banding the house horizontally under the eaves. On a house with a gabled roof, the frieze may be continued all around to form a break between the end walls and the gables. The frieze adds class and style. It is usually found on all but the most economically austere designs. The frieze may be as little as a 1 × 2 or as wide as a 1 × 12. It is installed with its face vertical. Where the ends are joined, a scarf cut is used. A scarf cut is a 45° end miter cut (a bevel). The corners are mitered also so that no end grain is exposed and the joint can be locked from both sides with nails.

Some builders prefer to install the frieze before the siding, leaving the lower nails unset. The last course of siding is then tucked under and the frieze nails are set permanently. There are some advantages to knowing precisely where the lower edge of the frieze will be in relation to the top of the door and window casings and to the overall vertical span of the siding. Other builders will dope these things out by measurement and go ahead with the siding first.

Like all lumber, the frieze is prone to shrinkage. There are two methods of combating the problem. Rub caulking into the end grain of each board as it is installed. This seals the most vulnerable part of the board, the open cells. Next, overlap each joint excessively, about $\frac{1}{32}$ to $\frac{1}{16}''$. Tap the nails again just before painting and the joint will tighten. If too much lap is allowed and the joint does not lie flush after tapping, a few passes with a plane will remove the high side.

Many illustrations show a rabbeted lower edge on a frieze board under which the siding is tucked. This is a rarity in actual practice. It is a feasible technique, but has two objectionable factors. First, no stock material exists with a ready-made rabbet to suit the need. Second, the depth of shadow line is cut down when up to half the board thickness is cut away at the edge for a rabbet.

Installing the frieze is done expediently without loss of time or thickness exposure by spacing the frieze out over the top edge of the last course of siding. This is readily accomplished with a horizontal strip behind the top part of the frieze, as was done under the bottom of the starter siding course. This strip is ripped to a thickness equal to the top siding board at the point of lap (Fig. 1-9). The lower edge of the frieze is lapped on top of the edge of the top siding course. A strip of the spacer material is tacked vertically behind each scarf joint and at all corners to provide a solid backup for nailing. The objective is to make the face of the frieze vertical.

THE STORY POLE

The siding boards should have equal and uniform exposure from bottom to top wherever it can be arranged. Some designs will call for a frieze board to top off the siding, whereas others will omit it. Regardless of which design is used, the exposure of each siding board and the consequent lap must be determined before starting the second course. Left to chance, the last course at the top will surely be unequal and present an obvious nonuniform exposure, a sign of amateurism.

Installing the Courses. The first course should be installed to overhang the foundation uniformly, about ½" to 1". This provides a rain drip edge so that water does not run back in under the wood sill. A soaked sill will lead to eventual decay, a condition called dry rot. It is prudent to seal the back of the first course with paint at least a couple of inches up from the bottom.

After the first course is installed, take a vertical measurement from the bottom edge to the bottom edge of the frieze or soffit (if there is no frieze) (*Fig. 1-10*). Divide the distance by a whole number that is one or two more than what it would take to cover

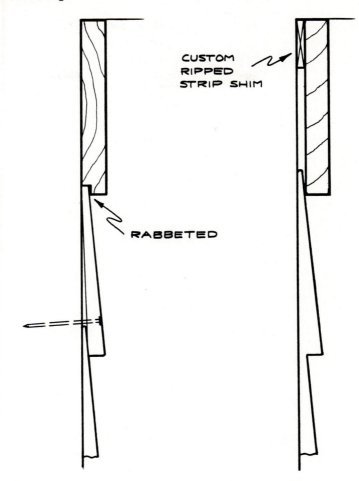

CUSTOM
RIPPED
STRIP SHIM

RABBETED

Figure 1-9 Frieze boards may be rabbeted to cover the top edge of horizontal siding or may be shimmed out in a vertical posture to lap over the siding.

the area with boards laid edge to edge. Take 12″ hardboard as an example. You have just measured and found the height to be 97½″. Eight boards would cover 96″. Nine boards laid edge to edge would net 108″ (97½″ from 108″ nets 10½″ of excess for lapping; 10½″ divided by 9 nets a single lap of 1.17″ or slightly under 1³⁄₁₆″).

Laying up each course by measuring the lap or the exposure each time will quickly compound any error, no matter how small. A good method of assuring parallelism and equal exposure of each board is to make and use a story pole for a guide, as masons

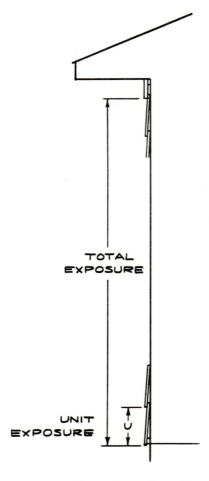

Figure 1-10 Graphic presentation of how to determine exposure and lap.

do. Cut a pair of 1 × 2s or 2 × 2s to a length a few inches longer than the distance from the bottom of the first board to the point where the siding exposure ends at the top. Nail a small block at the point that is the same as the overall siding exposure hei ght. Compute the exposure as per the example. On narrow bevel siding (4 to 6″), the lap should not be over 1″ or so for the sake of economy. On hardboard siding, any lap of more than 1″ or so will begin to create a crack under the edge due to the pivot angle, as a result of the absence of bevel on the face of the board. The corner of the top edge of each lower board becomes a fulcrum. When the lap is found to be too great or too small on the drawing board at the design stage, some adjustment can be worked out by varying the height of the frieze board. At construction time, the only alternative to excessive lapping is to cut down the height of the top course. With wide siding, an inch or two taken off will not be objectionable. Any more than that will cause a mismatch of the bevel parallelism and will be quite noticeable.

Transfer the exposure heights to the story pole, starting from the block to the other end (Fig. 1-11). This transfer must be superaccurate, ending at one end with a division precisely equal to the first. In this way, the pole can be used from either end. A sharp V notch cut with a knife or a straight slot cut shallowly with a handsaw will be seen better than a pencil mark.

Siding installation is basically a minimum two-person job. Even if one person does all the nailing, a helper is valuable to hold up the other end. The first course should be placed as perfectly straight as possible. Tack each board temporarily, leaving the nails exposed. Put a nail in each end and one in the center to pre-

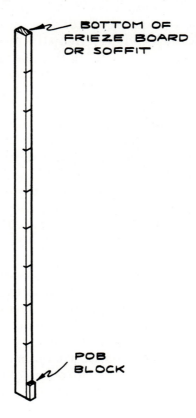

BOTTOM OF
FRIEZE BOARD
OR SOFFIT

POB
BLOCK

Figure 1-11 Story pole to match the problem cited in the text.

vent sagging. Put all the first course clear across a side of the house before starting any second-course parts. Use all the techniques of straightlining with string and sight. Place each nail so as to center through the starter strip and go on to anchor in the sill. Each nail will act as a guide for nails in boards above if it is placed directly below the center line of a stud. Do not nail at the top of the board. When the straightness of the first course is proven, proceed to locate and nail the second course. Check for straightness and parallelism. Make any necessary adjustment. Sink all nails.

Indexing with the story pole from this point on will assure uniformity and parallelism around the entire house. Hold a story pole at each end of a siding board and transfer the mark from the pole to the siding that is being lapped. Hook the story-pole block under the starter course. Mark another spot at the center point of medium-length board locations. Marks on approximate third points are advisable for long boards, which tend to sag considerably. A 16′ board, for example, could use three index marks, one at the beginning, one at 8′, and one at the end.

Place a nail in each end first. Go to the intermediate locations. Raise the board to the mark and nail it there. Remember to nail into the studs. Sight the lower edge to confirm straightness. Complete the nailing. Remember that all the nails should miss the board below, but be just above its edge.

One-person installation of siding is possible by placing a temporary, partially set nail in one of the index mark locations. This nail will support an end of the board resting on it while the carpenter nails the other end. After the board is nailed in several places, the temporary nail is removed and a dab of caulk pressed into the hole. Many of the shorter boards between windows can be handled without a supporting nail as they will wedge between the brickmolds enough to permit the first holding nail to be placed.

Joints.   Joint patterns on horizontal siding should be made as unobtrusive as possible. The same rule applies to horizontal siding as to other rain-shedding materials. The end joints from one course to the next are staggered. Also, do not line the joints up on every other course. Start at the bottom with the longest pieces available. Start the second course with a length that will end no closer than 4′ to the joint on the bottom course. Do not repeat the bottom course pattern in the third course, as this will begin to set up a jump course joint pattern, which attracts notice. One of the visual characteristics of early manufactured houses that were transported in two halves was a joint seam up the middle of the ends. This giveaway was soon eliminated by installing the siding on site or by using vertical siding. The objective is consciously to create a *random* pattern of end joints so that the eye is not drawn to any specific area of the wall. (Fig. 1-12).

As soon as breaks in the wall, windows, and doors are reached, it is often possible to span between them and to the house corners without joints. This should be done as much as possible. Save the cutoff ends for starters of a new course. Do not start a course with a piece under 32″ long, however. Save these short lengths to complete a run that happens to call for a short piece.

End-joint techniques vary with the material. Beveled wood siding, usually cedar, is cut and planed to butt perfectly square.

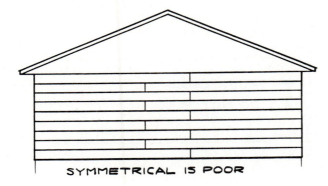

SYMMETRICAL IS POOR

RANDOM IS PREFERRED

Figure 1-12 Symmetrically arranged joints in the siding give prefabricated appearance. Randomly arranged appearance is preferred.

Rub some lead base caulk into the end grain and butt the interim joints tightly together.

Joints at the brickmold will perform as expansion joints for both wood and hardboard siding (Fig. 1-13). A gap of $\frac{1}{16}$ to $\frac{1}{8}''$ is left here. Rub caulk into the wood siding before nailing it on. Caulk the gap completely full after installation. Caulking must be pushed into the gap with the nose of the applicator pointed slightly in the direction of advance. Dragging the nozzle will only lay on a surface bead, with little or no penetration. The air must be forced out of the crevice ahead of the caulk. Also, unless you can see the caulk rolling down into the gap there is no assurance that it is penetrating.

Figure 1-13 Siding-to-trim junctions should be treated as expansion joints.

Latex and vinyl types of caulking make a more resilient expansion joint. Their life is also superior. When either of these two is used, it is better to rub the end grain with the same type of caulk that will be used to fill the gap. This will avoid the adhesion conflict of dissimilar materials.

Hardboard end joints should be accommodated in accordance with the manufacturer's instructions. A tight butt joint with this material will usually be the source of unending grief. The boards typically shrink and swell with the seasons. At times of high moisture, humidity, and many consecutive sunless days on end, the boards may swell and bulge between the nails. The pressure is so great at times that it will force the nails out. In hot, dry, sunny times, the boards shrink enough to open up cracks as wide as ¼″ between the ends of full-length boards and an ⅛″ at the laps.

Plastic joint strips are recommended for joining the ends of hardboard. The strip is shaped like the letter H in its cross section. A strip is slipped over the end of the siding board. Slip the next board into the strip and bottom it solidly (no gap). Mark a light line down both sides of the H strip on each board. Pull the unnailed board away from the strip until a total of ¼″ exists between the line(s) (it may all be on the new board side of the H strip). Nail the latest board. Tap the joint cover right or left until it is centered between the lines. The nails holding the ends of the two joined boards will require quite a bit of slant to reach the stud. It is important to locate accurately where the stud is, as the joint requires accurate centering. Even a slightly off center joint cover will probably cause a defective nail anchor on the short bearing side. Omit nailing the ends of each board at the joint until the cover strip has been centered. Be careful to avoid hitting the strip when driving the nails. Only one nail is used near the lower edge, the same as in the field. This system provides for lateral movement of the boards without exposing an objectionable crack at the joint during shrinkage times.

Butt joints that are unavoidable on long, uninterrupted surfaces must be arranged to end at the center of a stud unless wood sheathing exists for a nail base. With blackboard or Styrofoam sheathing, it is imperative that all siding nails anchor in a stud.

Notching the siding will be required at window locations. Seldom will the lower edge of a siding course coincide exactly with the bottom of a window sill. Even if it happens by design or coincidence, the board passing under the window will still require notching away the portion that would have been overlapped had there been no window.

Wooden casements usually have a groove or a rabbet under the sill in which to pocket the upper edge of the notched siding (Fig. 1-14). The siding is notched to seat most of the way into the groove. Approximately ⅛″ clearance above the groove is left for sealing. A bead of caulk is run into the groove, and the siding is pressed into the caulk to form an infiltration-proof and waterproof joint. Test the siding in the groove before spreading the caulk.

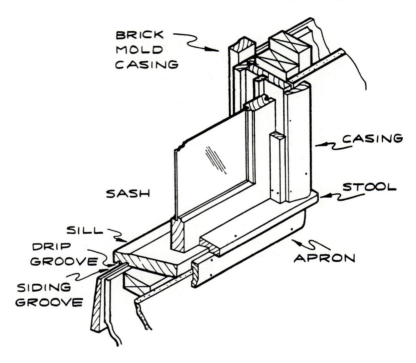

Figure 1-14 Window casements with an integral casing usually have a groove on the underside of the sill in which the top edge of the siding is pocketed.

MANUFACTURED SIDING

Vinyl, aluminum, and steel horizontal siding are all dependent on the first course for the straightness of the siding that will be placed above. On these manufactured types of siding, no nails will be ex-

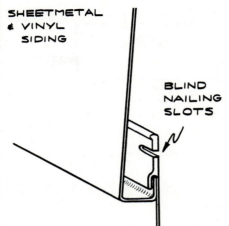

SHEETMETAL
& VINYL
SIDING

BLIND
NAILING
SLOTS

Figure 1-15 Aluminum and
vinyl siding is blind nailed in
slots made for the purpose.

posed (Fig. 1-15). On the upper edge there is a channel into which
the lower edge of the next piece hooks. Above the channel are perforated horizontal nailing slots. A nail is placed in each slot that
falls over a stud. Each nail is set lightly so that the slot will accommodate movement caused by expansion and contraction of the material.

Remodeling jobs where aluminum or vinyl is installed over
old siding require some preliminary preparation. Surrounds and
vertical furring strips are nailed on the walls. The furring strips do
not necessarily have to be on uniform centers to mate with the
nailing perforations, as these slots are continuous.

Nailing is unique. The manufacturer will recommend a nail
size that usually specifies a larger head. The nail is *not* seated
tightly. The head should be in contact with the sides of the slot but
only snug enough that the siding can stretch or shrink (Fig. 1-16).
The nail is placed near the center of the slot, or at least not touching the end of a slot. In this manner, the siding can adapt to temperature changes and move laterally without buckling or placing
undue stress on the nails.

End joints are generally lapped. A cutback area is provided at
the bottom and top of certain designs so that no misalignment of
the hook-in groove is created. Leave a small gap where the cutouts
meet so that this end of the siding piece will *not* butt the adjoining
piece and cause buckling. The manufacturer's installation instructions will indicate the recommended gap to be left. A new notch
will have to be cut when using a cutoff piece in a new course.

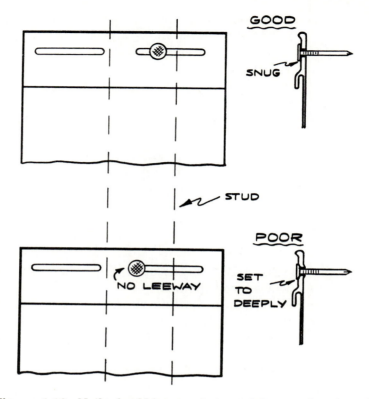

Figure 1-16 Nails should be snug but not tight enough to impede expansion and contraction of the siding.

The alignment of the base course is so important that it warrants emphasis. There is so little adjustment between the channel on the top edge and the hooking edge at the bottom that the first course must be laid nearly perfectly all around the house. The reward for this effort comes in the remainder of the job, which requires little attention to leveling and straightlining and therefore goes rapidly.

Cutting metal and synthetic siding is different from cutting wood or laminates. Sheet-metal blades are used in circular power handsaws. Some installers use a regular blade put on the saw backward to cut aluminum and vinyl (not steel). Surprisingly, the teeth, in the drag position, are not dulled by aluminum or vinyl any sooner than by wood.

Small circular saws are more effective and less dangerous than saws intended for woodwork. Intricate cuts not maneuverable with a circular saw can be made with a small saber saw (labeled, by some companies, a "jigsaw"). Wherever possible all cuts are made from the back side, which avoids marring the face. When a cut must be made from the face side, the finish of the siding should be protected with masking tape. Another system is to tape the base plate of the saw. Aluminum, magnesium, and steel base plates on saws will leave a dark gray mark on the surface of the siding if not masked.

Channels and J strips are used around windows and doors to pocket the ends and custom-cut edges of metal and synthetic siding. Preformed corners are available to contain the siding at inside and outside corner junctions. Where all the exposed wood is to be covered, the installation will start at the corners, followed by the window surrounds and then the siding, frieze, soffit, and facia.

A word of encouragement is timely. Aluminum and vinyl siding are not difficult to install. The success of a good job lies more in the area of attitude than manipulative skill. Two elements are important: (1) get started right, and (2) do not violate the principles of rain shedding. Leave no cracks open to weather or infiltration. Do not use butyl caulk as a substitute for good rain-shedding technique. Bend the first piece of trim (facia) to reach a corner, around the corner. Lap the adjacent piece to the corner. Use no corrosive or dissimilar metal nails. They will rust and cause unsightly blemishes. Do not nail through the face of trim if it is possible to nail from an underedge or hidden place. The do-it-yourselfer and the first-time builder can save a substantial amount of labor and franchise cost by installing manufactured sidings if the material is obtainable across the counter at reasonable unit prices. Kit and contract prices include a lot of costs other than labor.

VERTICAL SIDING

Vertical siding requires more forethought than horizontal siding, as the material is running parallel to the structural frame of most of the wall and therefore requires backing. An exception is the frame that is completely sheathed with plywood or waferboard.

Vertical siding is available in board sizes or in sheet form. Board-and-batten was an early system of covering that is still popular. Many spin-off designs are available in metal and synthetic material such as ribbed, grooved, and pressed contours.

Sheet siding is available in plywood, hardboard, and other composition materials. The standard width is 4'. Plywood comes in 8' and 9' lengths. The thickness of the sheet is often a determining factor in how the vertical edge joint is treated. Thin material usually has no joint and therefore requires a covering strip of some sort. Most plywood styles are $\frac{5}{8}$" thick and have a leading rabbet and trailing rabbeted edge.

BOARD-AND-BATTEN INSTALLATION

Rough-sawn cedar is a popular wood for vertical application. Tragically, many board-and-batten installations are nailed incorrectly. The result is long vertical cracks and splits that develop as a result of shrinkage from exposure to sun and high temperature.

The most common nominal board width in the board-and-batten system is 12". Most boards will vary from 11¼ to 11½". The "batts" are usually ripped from the same material. A generous and a less generous choice of batt width is possible. An 11¼" board ripped into four equal batts (three cuts) will net batts about 2⅝" wide. The same board ripped into five pieces (four cuts) will net batts about 2⅛" wide.

Successful nailing of the board is achieved by nailing only in the center of the board (Fig. 1-17). This permits swelling and shrinking to occur without stress to the soft grain of the wood. The boards are centered on a 1' spacing modulus regardless of any variance in actual width. The gaps between them will vary a little, but the exposure will be equal after the battens are installed. Install the batts on the boards 12" apart edge to edge. Mark the wall every 12" top and bottom. Center each board between the marks as you move down the wall.

Nailing the batten is the same as the boards, one nail only, midway between the edges. The batten nail does *not* go through the board underneath. It is a common *error* to suppose that a nail is needed on each edge to hold both the batten and the board firmly in place. This is a classic example of logic versus knowledge and experience. In this case, logic is theoretical and loses out to the forces of nature, shrinkage, and weak wood grain. Note carefully the illustrations showing the correct and incorrect nail locations.

Nail backing is mandatory for board-and-batten siding. Horizontal wood backing must be provided at least every 24" or less up

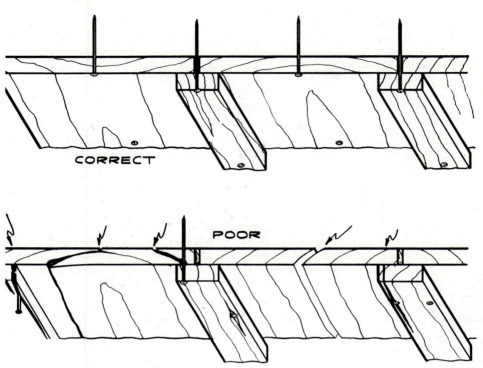

Figure 1-17 Board-and-batten siding must not be nailed next to the edges or through both boards. It should be nailed at the center so that it can shrink and swell without restriction from season to season.

the height of the wall. Blocks or bands of wood are traditional. Blocks between the studs are no longer a feasible method, as they interfere radically with insulating methods. Bands of 1 × 4s are still in use. Several innovative systems are practiced, always with the objective of leaving the wall core open for freedom of insulating with full blankets.

One backing method is to brace the corners diagonally with steel braces of the T or flat perforated type on the inside of the frame; then surface band the exterior with 1 × 4s top, bottom, and every 16″ or 24″ between. Short blocking between the bands is required on those studs where the vertical sheathing joints will be. The sheathing is then applied over the banding. Blackboard is the least costly sheathing. Styrofoam of ½ to ⅝″ thickness will improve the insulating quality considerably. Any greater thickness of Styrofoam will create a strain on the holding capacity of the batten nail that bridges the gap between the boards, as well as the Styrofoam. These two depths plus the batten thickness will be in excess of 2″ expended before the nail reaches the anchoring wood. This system mandates 16d galvanized casing or headed nails, both of which may be considered excessive in size for the nature of the trim (battens, corners, casing, frieze, etc.).

Another system is to sheath the frame first and then band it on the surface (Fig. 1-18). This provides a better nailing situation. Styrofoam sheathing must not be left exposed at the bottom, however, as it is vulnerable to insect and vermin infestation. A strip of wood surrounding the bottom, nailed to the sill, will solve this con-

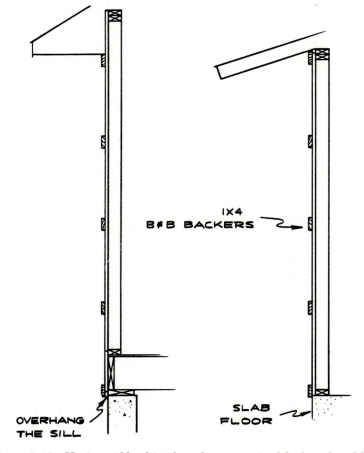

Figure 1-18 Horizontal backing boards are required for board-and-batten siding installation where soft sheathing is used.

dition. For a wood-framed floor, rip strips the same thickness as
the wall sheathing from precut stud stock (economy grade is
minimium-cost material), and nail each strip to the sill before
starting to sheath. The concrete slab floor has a combination sill/
sole on which part of the sheathing should be attached to avoid an
infiltration crack. The wood strip for this application is custom cut
to fit the need. The sheathing butts to the top edge of the strip.

A third backup banding method is to inlet three 1 × 4s into
the framing system before sheathing the wall (Fig. 1-19). The location for these boards is on quarter points, one-fourth up from the
sill, one-fourth down from the top plate, and one board centered between these. It is a feasible system if the inletting can be done
efficiently in a minimum of time with power tools. The sill plate
and the top plate provide the top and bottom backing.

The best method may be solid wood sheathing. An analysis
of labor time versus material cost may reveal that full-wall

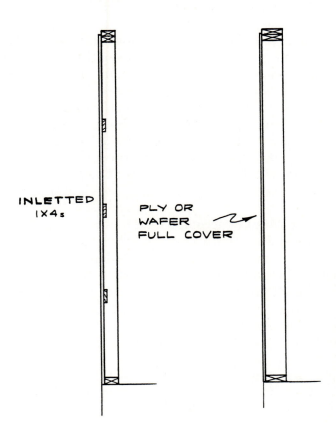

INLETTED
1×4s

PLY OR
WAFER
FULL COVER

Figure 1-19 Continuous
banding with 1 × 3 inletted
ribbons will not interfere too
much with the integrity of
blanket insulation and will
provide backup behind soft
sheathing for board-and-batten
siding. A full cover of plywood or
waferboard is good backup on
2 × 4 or 2 × 6 frame wall. No
other bracing required.

sheathing with ½″ CDX plywood or waferboard is as reasonable as any of the methods discussed previously. No banding or corner bracing is needed with the full-wall wood coverage. All the labor time for banding is eliminated. The building is superior in strength to the other systems involving soft sheathing. No diagonal corner bracing is required.

REVERSE BATTEN AND V-GROOVED SIDING

Sheet plywood wood siding is available in several patterns. A popular imitation of board-and-batten is called reverse batten. Instead of battens on the surface, this plyboard has relieved striations at intervals (12″ is most common), which create shadow lines giving off the appearance of battens. Other designs have grooves on closer spacing. Eight-foot sheets fit standard wall heights with precut studs on concrete slab floors. Nine-foot sheets adapt to standard walls on wood-framed floors.

Stud placement is critical if waste is to be avoided with sheet siding. The striated and grooved siding types are designed to be laid over studs placed on the 4′ modulus system; therefore, the stud spacing must be either 16 or 24″ OC. Once a sheet has been cut lengthwise (vertically), the unused side can only be used at the opposite end of the building or to start at another corner. The options for its use are very limited due to the rabbeted edges. The nominal width of the siding sheet is 4′; but the actual width is 48⅜″. The rabbet accounts for the additional ⅜″. The tongue of the leading edge is actually an extension of the striated batten groove (relief).

Placing the first sheet is accomplished by lining up the inner corner of the rabbet flush with the building line at a corner. Where the spacing of studs is correct in accordance with flush framing (Fig. 1-20) or setback framing (Fig. 1-21), this will place the lead tongue edge on the centerline of the 4′ modulus stud. Reverse-batten plywood siding may be nailed directly to the framework at a considerable saving. In this case, the frame must be flush with the building line so that the siding can hang below the top of the foundation.

Flanged-type windows adapt fairly well to vertical siding where the window is sheltered by an overhanging eave. A simple casing can be surface nailed around the window on top of the sid-

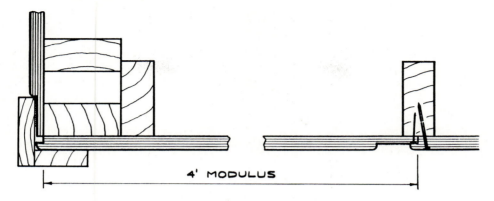

Figure 1-20   Reverse board-and-batten plywood siding applied directly to the wall frame.

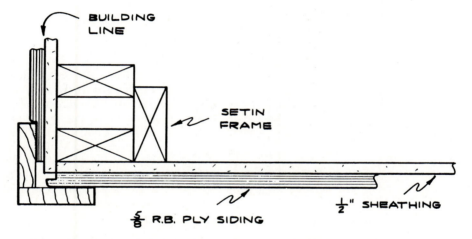

Figure 1-21   Reverse board-and-batten applied over ½″ sheathing with 1 × 4 corner trim.

ing. Like other wood siding, a clearance gap of about ⅛″ is left between the siding and the window jamb for caulk sealing. The sill trim piece can be a two-piece design with a sill board at a slant of about 15 to 20° supported underneath by a surface board with a corresponding bevel on the top and bottom edges (Fig. 1-22). The side casings will butt on top of the sill board with a corresponding end bevel. The top board will be beveled on the lower edge. This board will meet the frieze board on its top edge. Where the frieze is at a higher level (soffit on the rake), a drip cap piece like the sill is an attractive capping piece (Fig. 1-23).

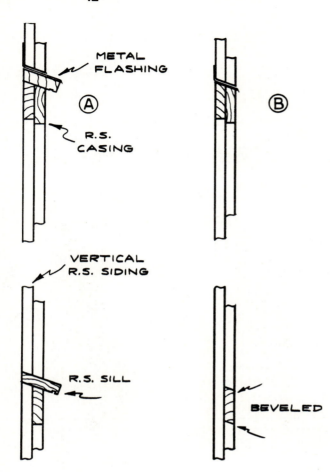

Figure 1-22 A dripcap and sill are needed where there is no eave protection above a window or door opening as on the gable ends of a house (A). Where such openings are adequately protected, a simple flat casing may suffice, as in (B). In both styles the use of flashing at the top is a must.

A **simpler casing** involves no more than a picture-frame-type of surface-mounted set of four boards. The top corners may be mitered or butted (side board under top board). The bottom corners are usually butted, side boards on top of the bottom board. The bottom board should always have at least the top edge beveled to shed water away from the crack under the window jamb sill. Caulk this joint while installing the board.

Windows not sheltered by eaves present a special problem with sheet siding. Slovenly builders are inclined to ignore the water-shedding requirement at the top and simply caulk the upper edge of a surface-mounted casing board. Such a joint will ultimately fail. Water will get under the siding and begin the deterioration process. The striations in the siding form particularly vul-

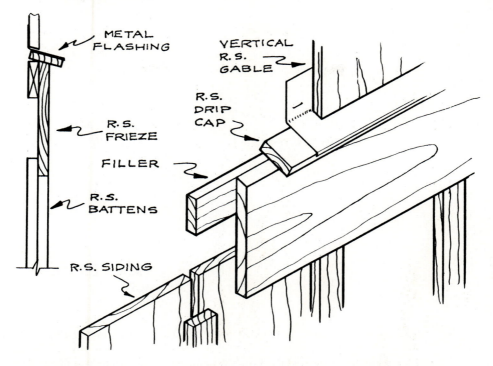

Figure 1-23   The same kind of drip cap used on windows and doors may be used on top of a frieze board on a gable end of the house.

nerable pockets for water retention. One of two systems of fabricating a drip cap is necessary. The first method uses ripped and beveled components of rough-sawn lumber. The second method employs a drip-cap molding such as that used with brick molding (Fig. 1-24). To be foolproof, both methods require flashing that extends up behind the siding.

BRICK VENEER SIDING

Brick facing on a house is called *veneer* where it simply screens a surface and bears no substantial weight of the structure. The basic framing of a house is the same for a veneered house as it is for a house sided with other forms of siding. The differences arise from the dimensional decisions at the designing stage and from the manner in which the brick is blended with the trim of the house.

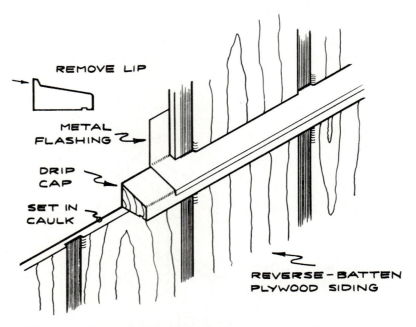

Figure 1-24 A stock dripcap molding may be used below vertical sheet siding, as well as for horizontal lap siding for which it was designed. The upper setout lip must be removed for smooth flashing.

Design characteristics of siding a house with brick should be considered and determined on the drawing board. The question is whether the modularity of a structure should be based on the framing modulus or on the masonry units. There are several considerations that will lead to the conclusion that a structurally wood framed house should adhere to the modules of wood (the plywood sheet), the basic 4′ unit. Older traditional bricks were mainly standardized on a 4″ × 8″ modulus. Recent mass-produced units of 3″ × 10″ size and others have altered the modularity picture as far as brick is concerned. Actually, there is no longer a significant basis on which to consider brick modularity. There is, however, a basis to maintain modularity coinciding with the concrete block modulus (8 × 16″). A block building faced with brick is best designed with its exterior block line dimensions divisible by 8″. It follows logically that any structure employing a block foundation, with or without wood framing, will best adapt to both masonry and wood when the dimensions fit the 8″ and 4′ moduli.

The basis for this reasoning lies in the nature and adaptability of the materials to alteration. One would think that wood is easier to reduce to custom size than a masonry unit. In a sense this is true. It is easier to cut and use one-third of a sheet of plywood than to cut and use one-third of a concrete block (especially if it is a two-hole block). On the other hand, it is not at all difficult to split bricks into thirds by trowel or by diamond masonry saw. There is great logic, then, to coordinating the blocks and plywood into dimensional units that will eliminate or minimize the cutting of either in a specific design. For example, a $28 \times 44'$ house dimension is erected with all whole units of blocks in the foundation and full sheathing units on the frame walls. In addition to the ease of assembly, there is the reward of minimum waste. In reality, one can have greater square footage in the plan at little or no extra cost. Astute tract builders have practiced this concept of labor and material conservation since World War II with great economic success. The conclusion is that the brick-veneered house plan will benefit most by planning the framework around the moduli of $16''$ and $48''$.

The application of brick veneer to a frame shell will be cause for coordinated designing of the footing, a brick ledge, brick pockets (built-out frieze), and an overhanging gable wall to form a brick pocket. The brick pockets are all part of the carpenter's work. In the sequence of construction, these woodwork features are constructed before the bricklaying. All casing around doors and windows is installed, and brick pockets are formed and preferably painted or stained before the mason begins. This permits the mason to drop lines and story poles from the exact corners where the brick will contact the frieze board. It permits the grouting of all contact points with mortar so that there will be no openings between the masonry and the adjoining materials. Like most building materials, there will be a small amount of shrinkage, which creates a little crack of these junctions. A thorough caulking job after the structure has stabilized is the final sealing step.

Brick pocket depth is dependent on the brick size specified. Pocket depths can be made with stock materials that will fit most situations. For example, a pocket can be made with 2×4 blocks on edge with a 1×4 nailed flat to the lower end of these 2×4 drops. These drops are toenailed to the top plate and each stud. The frieze board is nailed to the drops and to the edge of the 1×4 (2×4s are excellent also for the lower backup, where cost permits). The frieze should hang below the pocket drop about $2''$ to give the mason some room to lift the last course of brick (soldier course) up into the

pocket and lower each brick into the mortar. The $3\frac{1}{2}''$ pocket made
in this manner will accommodate the 3″ brick that is so popular
(Fig. 1-25). The actual depth of this brick is a full 3″, so a "finger
space" cavity of $\frac{1}{2}''$ will separate the brick from the sheathing.
This is about the minimum that masons care to work with, since
any bulge or misalignment of the frame wall could reduce the gap
so much that it would require the entire veneer wall to be set out
farther. No mason will lay an unstraight wall by choice.

Deeper pockets can be formed by varying the assembly
methods. A $4\frac{1}{4}''$-deep pocket results from placing two 1 × 4s or
1 × 2s behind the 2 × 4 drops. This design is readily assembled at
ground level in sections and raised. When done this way, offset the
blocks so that they are right or left (uniformly) of the stud locations. When raised in place, the assembly is attached by nailing
through the backing boards into the studs and plate. Deeper
pockets can be shimmed out in other ways. To accommodate 6″
stone veneer, a pocket is made by using 2 × 6 blocks ($5\frac{1}{2}''$ actual)
backed with the 1 × 4s, for a total $6\frac{1}{4}''$. To up it to $6\frac{3}{4}''$, a shim of

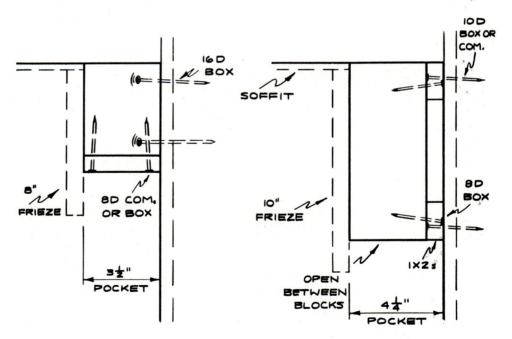

Figure 1-25   Typical brick pocket designs for actual 3″ size brick and nominal 4″ size brick.

½" plywood can be used continuously or single pieces can be tacked to each drop.

A problem can arise around the windows. Whatever the pocket system chosen, the back side of the bricks must not be farther from the sheathing surface of the wall than the thickness of the window and door casing. Brick molding is made from "five quarter" stock and measures 1⅛" deep from most mills. A ½" space behind the bricks will leave about ⅝" of brick touching this wood molding, which is adequate for grouting and caulking. Rough-sawn casing will range from ¾" to ⅞" thick, which reduces the brick-to-wood contact. Keep the casing depth in mind when designing the pocket. Incidentally, those builders aspiring to be professionals will benefit by knowing that the mason will judge the quality of the house by the straightness of the pockets and walls and the plumbness of the openings. The word gets around.

Gable setout is the other major adaptation required of the carpenter whose house will be brick sided up to the gable. This style will coordinate the brick pocket with a hung-over gable. The entire gable framework (all cripple studs) will extend beyond the sheathing below whatever distance is required to form a pocket. The support of this overhang should not depend on toenails alone. A minimum of three studs of 2×8 size is needed to support the gable (Fig. 1-26). These are notched at the bottom to bear on the top plate. They are notched at the top on the same interior edge to receive the rafters when an overhang is planned. These 2×8 notched gable studs transfer the weight of the gable directly to the end wall.

On a trussed gable the brick pocket frieze backer studs can be supported adequately by nailing through the flat gable studs from the interior side into the pocket studs (Fig. 1-27). The nails through these supports should slant slightly upward to gain all the shear support possible. The pocket studs will hang down below the plate line the same amount as the pocket blocks under the horizontal eaves around the corners so that a uniform transition level passes around the corner with both the brick and the frieze board.

A molded drip cap is needed above the frieze board on the gable ends. For rough-sawn and/or vertical siding, a drip cap can be fabricated by ripping a parallel bevel on each edge of a 1×4 or 1×3. This style requires a metal flashing strip running up behind the siding. Asphalt-impregnated building paper cut in 4" strips is sometimes used but will not last as long as aluminum (Fig. 1-23).

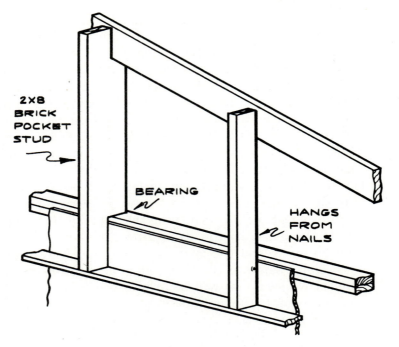

Figure 1-26 A traditional stick-built gable needs three or more notched setout studs that bear on the top plate to support the other studs, which are supported only by nails. The exterior face of the rafter and the sheathing are on the same vertical line.

A brick-faced gable will be treated with a pocket under the rake overhang of the eave. This pocket will be constructed something like the horizontal frieze pocket if it is a high pocket (6″ or more). Where a minimum pocket is adequate, it can be formed simply with a flat 2 × 4 and covered with a 1 × 4 rake frieze board. The soffit is installed first. Then a 2 × 4 is nailed to the soffit and into the soffit backer. The frieze is then nailed to the vertical edge of the 2 × 4. This nets a pocket height perpendicular to the rake of 2″, which is barely enough to contain a square brick end. Some larger bricks will require mitering of the corner of each brick. A 1 × 6 is a more attractive and more desirable rake frieze to the mason, as it will pocket any face brick without cutting.

A brick sill is another item that requires the attention of the builder and the consumer. Bricks laid on edge perpendicular to the wall under a window sill or door sill or on top of a wainscot wall (a partial height wall) are in a formation known as *rowlock*. In these

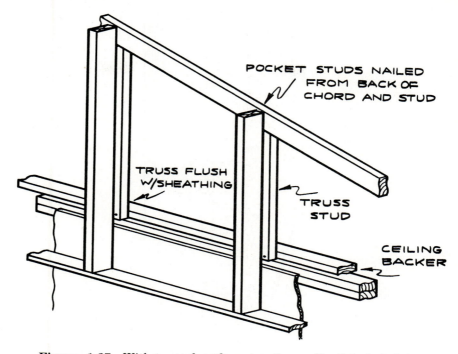

POCKET STUDS NAILED
FROM BACK OF
CHORD AND STUD

TRUSS FLUSH
W/SHEATHING

TRUSS
STUD

CEILING
BACKER

Figure 1-27 With trussed roof construction and/or flat stud placement, the brick pocket frieze backer can be nailed from behind the stud for adequate support.

three locations the rowlock course *must* be slanted to shed the rain away from the building. The greater the slant is, the more successful will be its function. The bricks will need to be cut, as a full-length brick of the shortest kind will hang over too far. The cantilever rule for corbeling applies to overhangs. The codes limit a masonry corbel or cantilever to 25 percent of the length of the unit. More than a one-fourth overhang exposes the brick to too much end leverage. It is more easily damaged or broken loose from its mortar bond. Sills with no slant or inadequate slant permit water to convect back under the window and door sill and cause deterioration of the materials. The house buyer should monitor the existence of a proper-sill detail in the plans and during construction.

Wainscots require flashed junctions above the rowlock cap (Fig. 1-28). The flashing must go up behind the siding above the brick cap and extend on to the brick far enough to prevent water from penetrating behind the brick wall.

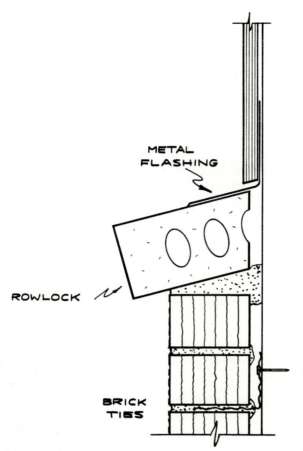

METAL
FLASHING

ROWLOCK

BRICK
TIES

Figure 1-28 Flashing is a must behind siding that drains onto rowlock-laid brick veneer. Note the metal brick tie. One is required for every 2′ of brick coverage vertically and horizontally.

Weep holes are required in all exterior exposed brick veneer walls. A weep hole is a small hole or slot as large as the mortar joint at the intersection of a horizontal and vertical brick joint. Its purpose is to drain condensed water and moist air from between the brick and frame walls. The hole should be located in a course level below the first wood member of the house (the sill), but in a course that is above the level of the surrounding ground. Flashing is run up the face of the wood framing before sheathing is installed. It is bent out on top of the course of brick below where the "weeps" will be (Fig. 1-29). The sheathing is installed over the vertical part of the flashing. In designs where sheathing paper is used on the face of the sheathing, the flashing may be surface nailed to the sheathing. The first course of building paper is lapped over the flashing to form the watershed. The next course of brick will be

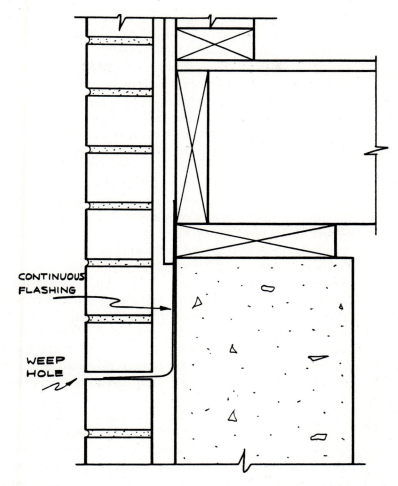

CONTINUOUS
FLASHING

WEEP
HOLE

Figure 1-29   Weep holes in a masonry veneer wall are necessary to
allow moisture from condensation to escape.

laid on top of the flashing, with mortar under and over the
flashing. Bricks with holes must have the holes completely covered
by the flashing. The flashing must not reach or protrude beyond
the outer face. Some brick-to-brick contact is necessary to create a
bond between the courses.

Masons have various ways of forming the weep. Some will
simply leave out the vertical joint at intervals of 4′ or less (the
maximum between weeps). Others will place a steel dowel in the
joint, grout around it, and ease it out later with a revolving

motion. The latter method does not permit the placement of a screened vent as required in many locales. Regardless of the method, it is important to keep the passageway open to waterflow. Punching a hole through after the bricks have been laid does not work, as the mortar is compressed between the brick and the wall where it forms an effective dam. The water will then stand between the weeps and ultimately break down the flashing.

Sill sloping, correct overhang, and adequate weeps with flashing are three items of sufficient importance to write them into your masonry contract. Be very specific. The author has appeared as an expert witness in several lawsuits where these factors were in contention. Each case was won, appealed, and won again by the consumer on the basis of substandard construction practice. The result of the absence of weep holes, incorrectly flashed cap courses, and inadequately sloped sills and porches was evident in rotted floor sills, door sills, window sills, and floor headers behind porches. The carpeting was moldy. There was even evidence of abnormally high respiratory affliction to the occupants due to the dampness in the house in all seasons. In this particular case the owner was awarded a sum equal to about one-third the cost of the total construction contract. The entire matter could have been avoided with adequate consumer knowledge, a specific contract (written specifications included), and some critical-stage surveillance.

Brick ties, because they are hidden from view, are sometimes overlooked or ignored. A brick tie is a small strip of rippled and galvanized sheet metal about $3/4 \times 6''$ with several nailing holes (Fig. 1-30). The tie is nailed to the wall through the sheathing into a stud. Most building codes call for ties throughout the wall on not greater than 24'' spacing apart from each other, both horizontally and vertically. Usually, the ties are placed from the bottom starters to as high as the installer can reach all around the building before brick laying commences. The remaining high ties are installed after scaffolding is in place. The ties are nailed flat to the wall and bent into the course joint on top of the wet mortar.

Brick ties are not intended to be structural devices; they will not hold brick to wood or wood to brick without adequate foundation under both. The ties *will* provide some lateral strength derived from the uniting of the two walls. The brick veneer will be considerably relieved of any tendency to teeter on its narrow base and fall away from the top of the frame wall. Foundation shifting

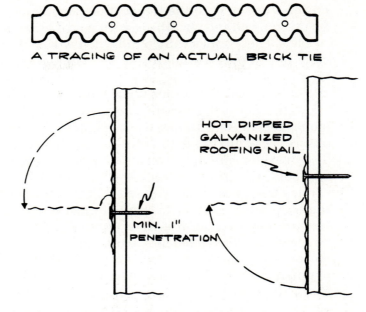

A TRACING OF AN ACTUAL BRICK TIE

HOT DIPPED
GALVANIZED
ROOFING NAIL

MIN. 1"
PENETRATION

Figure 1-30 Brick ties may be pulled down or up into the mortar joint. (*Note*: Brick ties shown above have been reduced.)

from any cause will not have the calamitous effect on a tied wall that is characteristic of the collapse seen where no ties exist. Brick ties are beneficial and well worth the minimal cost. They should never be omitted.

STONE SIDING

Tying stone to a wall requires a different order of tie installation. Coursed stone permits ties to be prenailed in a horizontal line over a large portion of the wall initially. Irregular-shaped stone and stone of nonuniform height will not permit prenailing of the ties, as many of them will not coincide with the joint locations. To tie irregular stone veneer, each tie must be nailed individually at an appropriate bonding level. This calls for much more attention to monitoring of the locations of previously attached ties. These ties, now hidden from sight, must be recorded in some way to assure that the 24″ minimum spacing rule is followed. Masons develop their own techniques. Some depend on memory (not often satisfactory). One simple method is to place a small piece of masking tape on the stone next to the tie location. Another method is to mark a future zone on the sheathing with a crayon where the next will be needed. These zones can be indicated with a 6″ oblong mark vertically placed over a stud (Fig. 1-31). The top of the oblong is the extremity of the boundary. As soon as a tie is installed somewhere in the oblong mark, another oblong zone is marked above.

The basic responsibility for proper tying lies with the brick or stone mason. As with much of the hidden structure of a project, the assurance of quality details will be on the shoulders of an overseer. The overseer may be a consumer who is knowledgeable, or a professional who has been assigned the authority. Regardless of who carries the responsibility to see that this type of job is done according to specifications (or to code), it must be monitored at the actual time of construction. It is *never* good business to get there late and be forced to take someone's word that, "Oh yes, the steel is in the footing just like you want it," or "Actually, I always make a habit of putting more ties in than necessary just to be on the safe side." You will never really know unless you see for yourself at the time

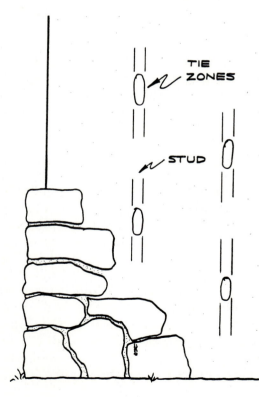

Figure 1-31 Masonry ties for a face-stoned veneer wall are indexed and nailed one at a time within 24″ of the last one.

of construction or find out the hard way at a later date when something breaks down. The recent popularity of metal detectors has made it possible to confirm the existence of ties. If none are found *after* a wall is complete, the next decision will be a difficult one to face.

PAINTING ADVICE

In this text a lot of emphasis has been placed on the necessity to preserve wood at the construction site. Much attention has been focused on the nature of wood to swell, shrink, and deteriorate. It is always advisable to seal all forms of trim wood as soon as installed. The longer the delay is, the more the wood is apt to warp.

Another reason to prime, paint (or stain), and finish is present when masonry veneer siding is used. The best sequence is to have all wooden trim finished before beginning the masonry. Painting with a brush will go much faster when one does not have to be careful about runovers or drips onto brick or stone. Paint may be sprayed on, for those who prefer this method, before masonry is installed without fear of overspray.

A final reason for trimming first is compelling. Mortar bonding in its fluid state is readily molded to the junctions between brick and wood. Reversing this sequence would cause much contour sawing where edges meet masonry. Visualize wood siding, a sheet of reverse board-and-batten, for example, being custom fitted to the vertical sides of a fieldstone fireplace.

Installing a frieze board after the brick is up would be unwise. Pounding on the frieze will break the bricks loose from their mortar bond more often than not. The mortar bond does not reach its ultimate strength until the twenty-eighth day. Even after that time, it takes very little shock to crack a bond on the top course. It is clear for many reasons that all trim that contacts or is close to masonry should be installed before the mason is called in.

PHILOSOPHY OF EXTERIOR COMPLETION

Ethics and practicality walk hand in hand when building the basic structural parts of a house. The structure must be strong enough to be safe under normal stresses and strong enough to provide a reasonable margin of safety during abnormal stress times. A caring and thoughtful builder will demonstrate responsibleness by including the little extras that protect against wind storms, tornadoes, and hurricanes. Those interested only in making money are always tempted (and frequently succumb) to shortcutting where elements are hidden from view.

The exterior finish of a structure does not provide much opportunity for economizing. Where the finishing touches are plain, austere, or lacking entirely, the appearance is so obvious that it will downgrade an asking price. Therefore, a quality job of finishing usually is worth the expense, as it will pay back at initial sale or resale time.

The consumer should be aware that a lot of flashy attractive finish on and in a house is not a reliable indicator of out-of-sight quality. An exposed aggregate driveway (washed granite stone), for example, is attractive—until it cracks. The underlying concrete requires special reinforcing techniques if cracks are to be reliably avoided. The best quality paint available on a house will be of little value if the material under it has not been protected by adequate condensation and moisture-proofing techniques. High-quality cabinets will be wasted on walls that are warped and prone to cracks due to the inadequate basic structure of the house frame. The list goes on and on. Truisms bear repeating. Good-quality builders work steadily throughout their lifetime. Shortcutters are prone to work stoppage and bankruptcy, not to mention lawsuits and forced vocational changes. The consumer is usually the best advertiser the builder can have. There is no substitute for quality construction and builder integrity.

Review Topics

1. Explain in detail how to install a window with an integral casement.
2. How is an opening made ready for window installation where soft nonstructural sheathing is used?
3. Describe the key locations for shims and filler blocks around a door jamb.
4. Give the standard hinge spacing and placement for two- and three-hinge passage doors.

5. Explain how one "locks" a mitered corner of brick molding.

6. What usually happens to cedar siding of the traditional beveled type when it is mistakenly nailed at the bottom and top (through the lapped part)?

7. Describe a method of installing frieze boards that will not require a special edge to be cut.

8. The lap of bevel siding or hardboard plank siding should be in a range of 1 to 2″. Explain fully how to cause it to be in this lap range and have all pieces equally exposed.

9. Describe how to make a story pole for a specific siding job.

10. Explain how to caulk between brickmold and the ends of siding around a window in order to have a long-lasting job.

11. Describe the correct way to nail board-and-batten siding. Include an explanation of the consequences of incorrect nailing.

12. Describe three optional methods of providing wood backup for nailing board-and-batten siding.

13. Explain how to place the first sheet of reverse board-and-batten plywood directly on a frame wall.

14. Describe how to prefabricate and assemble at ground level a brick pocket frieze backer section that will be hoisted and nailed as a unit to the wall.

15. Cite the regulation for brick ties and describe how to install brick ties for both brick and face stone-veneered walls.

PART 2

INTERIOR COMPLETION

5 PRINCIPLES OF UTILITY INSTALLATION

There are many hidden things behind the interior wall skin of a house. Common items found in most modern structures are plumbing pipes for water supply, venting, and drainage, electrical wiring for telephones and electrical outlets of several types, and heating ducts to carry hot air into the rooms and others to return the air to the heating plant. Other popular conveniences such as cable TV and central vacuum systems require hidden components. Also, of course, there is the little door chime wire to remember.

To properly conceal these utilities behind the walls, the location of each must be carefully planned in advance. Leaving such locations to chance or to the habitual design of a subcontractor will probably result in shortages in places of need.

The jobs of plumbing, heating, cooling, and wiring involve skills that are within the realm of the amateur if adequate self-education is undertaken. Those ambitious and courageous enough to tackle these trades will do well not to try to get all the required information that is necessary by word of mouth. One should first search out and read reliable books on the subject to gain a basic knowledge and a grasp of the terminology. The next step is to contact the local building authority office and obtain information about codes and permits. Many municipalities will not permit an unlicensed person to install the three basic utilities unless under the auspices of a licensed contractor in the specific trade. When this second step is accomplished, it is time to get back into the research and plot your course in depth.

It is not the purpose of this text to teach the specifics of plumbing, heating, or wiring. This is left to the many good books that are to be found. A word of caution will be useful. Before purchasing a costly book, take the time to look through it carefully. Write down some pertinent questions concerning specific installation situations and then test the book to see if answers are there. Many books are attractive but only theoretical. When a problem arises on the job, you will need a manual with good, clear answers and illustrations.

The intent of the following sections is to point out a few guidelines toward basic principles that are tried and true. Whether one tackles the job hands-on or subcontracts it, it will be advantageous to know what has proved to be efficient.

The order of utility installation is important to some extent. Large items that would be hard to redirect or alter should be placed first. This would include such things as ductwork and ridged piping. Next will come the more flexible items, such as electrical wiring, telephone lines, and cable TV circuits. Finally, there is the soft insulation and a vapor barrier. Now the hidden core of the house is ready for a wall-covering skin.

☐ PLUMBING

There are choices to be made in the plumbing materials to be used in the walls. There are two categories for pipe selection. One system involves hot and cold water supply. The other system involves drain and vent piping. Supply pipes in the wall will usually all be of ½″ size. Some ¾″ pipe will be used from the source to the water heater and to the first branch lines in the cold and hot circuits. This sizing helps to maintain pressure when more than one faucet is on at the same time. A trunk line or manifold setup is advisable where several outlets are anticipated to be in operation simultaneously on a frequent basis. Changes in direction are made by using 45 or 90° sweated-on elbows (soldered). Hard copper is usually used in crawl space houses and houses with basements where it can be run in straight lines and joined with couplings and elbows.

Soft copper comes in 50′ or longer rolls. It is usually mandated in slab-floor installations that carry a "no joint" regulation. Joints are made only above the floor. Soft copper can be bent quite easily to change direction. Care must be taken to avoid crimping the pipe. Once crimped, a high probability of leakage exists. Such flattening will also cause a reduced flow of water through the pipe. Benders are available that minimize crimping and make sharper bends possible.

VENTING

Drain and vent pipe size is regulated by code. The size ranges from 1¼″ inside diameter to 4″. There are two thicknesses of synthetic drain pipes. The heavier thickness (about ¼″) is used inside the house. The lighter weight (about ⅛″) is used outdoors where permitted. Most codes permit 3″ main drains when made of synthetics. The size and quantity of dry vent pipes (those carrying no water) is also conditioned by the distance from the vented facility. For example, a tub, lavatory, and commode may all be vented from a common "stack" if the drains in each are within a certain minimum horizontal distance from the stack.

All vents should be "roughed in" to the wall cavities before any part of the wall is covered. Water supply pipes can be brought in through the walls or through the floor. A few more elbows are required for the wall-entrance location. Even so, this location is preferred, as it eliminates drilling through vanity and kitchen cabinetry shelves under the sinks. The floor-entry method is easier, however, for remodeling jobs where a sink is located in a new spot.

Slant vents and drains a little in the direction of flow (Fig. 2-1). All horizontal drain pipes should have a little drop toward the vertical stacks into which they flow in order to empty out completely. Long, horizontal drains, particularly the main septic carrier, should be pitched to fall at a rate of ⅛″ to the foot. More than this will sometimes run the water off too rapidly, leaving solid waste behind. Any less than ⅛″ per foot will not provide adequate movement for all the contents. Be careful not to allow the pipe to sag anywhere lest the contents stand and create a blockage.

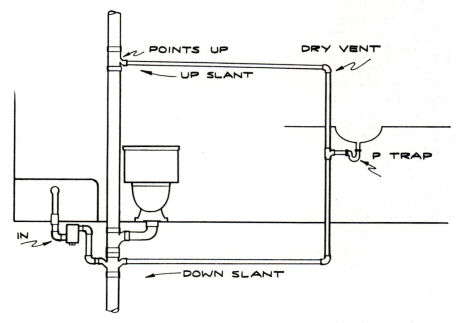

Figure 2-1 A typical one-wall drain system. Lavatory is revented because it is too far from the main stack (dry vent). Tub is shown "wet vented." Regulations differ.

Dry vents carry gas and odors out the top. Any "horizontal" portion of a dry vent should slope up a little as it travels toward its vertical vent pipe. This will permit the warm air to pass quickly up and away.

Water supply pipes require no pitch, as the water in them is under pressure and not affected by gravity. Hot and cold pipes should be kept apart from each other about 4 to 8″ so that the hot and the cold water radiation are isolated from each other.

Wood butchering should be avoided. Major structural components such as floor and ceiling joists should never have their strength reduced by excessive notching or notching in the wrong place. There are rules in the building code books pertaining to notching. Good sense mandates adhering to these rules faithfully. Drill a hole instead of notching wherever possible. Where notching is the only possible way to place a pipe, be sure to bring the notched board back to its original strength by reinforcing it (Fig. 2-2). Nail a splice alongside. A splice on a joist that does not reach the bearing points will be significantly more effective where glued

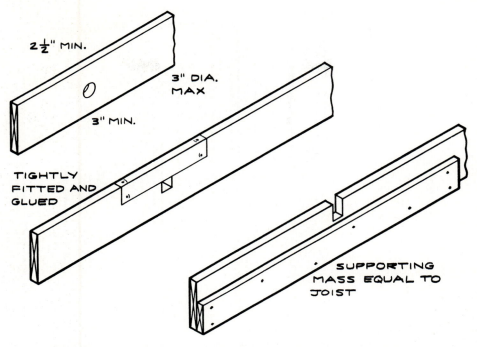

Figure 2-2 Holes for plumbing drilled through structural lumber detract the least from strength. Notched joists should be reinforced in one or both ways shown.

as well as nailed. If a joist requires near or complete severing, it will be best to install headers, following the same rules as those for openings in a floor.

A nifty bathroom wall design that eliminates notching completely is one framed with a 2 × 6 sole and top plate. Wherever a horizontal vent is located, pairs of 2 × 4 studs are placed flat, leaving a 2″ clear passage between. A 2″ spacer board is positioned horizontally above the pipe between the studs. One nail through each stud into this board will produce a stiff, straight, and flat wall surface. No holes or notches are required for the vent pipe that passes between the flat pairs of studs on its way to the main stack (Fig. 2-3).

Another method of reventing, as this is called, is to run the sink vent vertically through the top double plate into the attic and there cross over to connect to the main stack vent. There is a structural disadvantage in this design. The top double plate must be cut or drilled. Where the plate runs at right angles (crosses) the ceiling

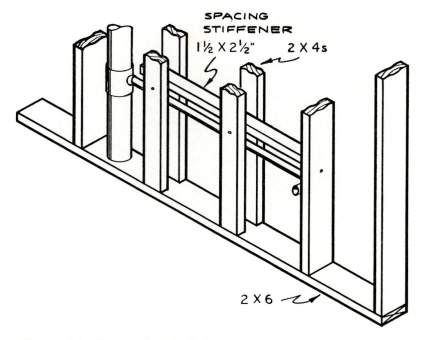

Figure 2-3   Flat stud method of providing for horizontal drain and vent pipes.

joist, the weakening is not significant, as a joist on each side of the hole will be firmly toenailed to the plate. Where the partition runs parallel and between two joists, some special attention should be given to firming up the weakened plate. This can be accomplished by positioning a 2 × 4 ceiling block on each side of the hole. Lay these blocks flat on the plate and nail through the ceiling joists into the ends of the blocks. Surface nail the blocks to the plate after checking the straightness of the partition. The same method can be used with a single 2 × 8 or larger drilled block. Center the width of the block over the pipe hole in the partition. Nail it in place, avoiding the hole location with the nails. From the underside, place the hole saw in the hole in the plate and proceed to drill through the block for a perfectly aligned hole. Attention must be directed to drilling in as nearly perfect a vertical direction as possible. The hole in the latter method will be passing through 4½″ of wood. Even a slight cant may cause a problem in placing the vent pipe.

Metal protector plates will eliminate concern about puncturing the pipe with dry wall nails (Fig. 2-4). Any type of sheet iron that will not be punctured by a nail may be used. The length of the metal plate should be about 2″ longer than the diameter of the pipe it protects. For the sole, it needs to be as wide (high) as whatever amount of sole is exposed above the underlayment flooring. For the top plate, a single piece, 2½″ wide (high), or two of the bottom size pieces are needed. The 2½″ plate is aligned with the lower edge of the double-top plate. The ceiling board takes up the upper ½″. Mortice the wood with a chisel, half-hatchet, or a router a little deeper than the metal plate thickness. The added depth will accommodate the nailheads that will protrude above the metal.

INDEXING PVC

A unique feature of PVC pipe can cause great consternation and waste for the novice plumber. The pipe joints are fastened with a solvent that sets almost instantaneously. There is no way to disassemble a PVC joint once the solvent has been applied and the two pieces pushed together. A misaligned joint can only be sawed off and thrown away.

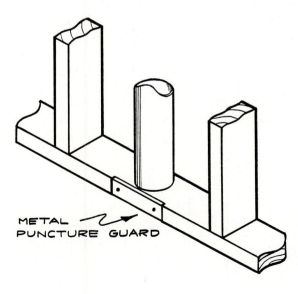

METAL
PUNCTURE GUARD

Figure 2-4 Metal guards of about ⅛″ × 1 ½″ are inletted in front of pipes and vents to prevent puncture from drywall or baseboard nails.

The best assembly routine is to index the exact position of each elbow, T, Y, or bend (Fig. 2-5). Start the process by fitting each piece dry. When a pipe is cut, chamfer the inside edge with a half-round file or rough sandpaper so that the water will flow freely. Chamfer the outer edge a little, removing all scraggly chips so that the pipe will press into the joint opening smoothly. Start the assembly at the main drain source and work up and out like the trunk and limbs of a tree. Work toward the end of the vents above the roof. After large segments of the system are fitted and assembled, each joint is indexed with a line passing at a right angle across the junction of the two pieces to be joined. Where there are several joints of the same kind and size, place a matching number on each piece at the point of indexing. Remember the flow direction. All Ys that drain downward will position to slope downward. All Ys in the dry venting posture will slant up. This Y is upside down. In a one-story house, this will include all the dry-vent Ys above the sinks. This is an important detail, as a reversed Y will not carry the odors out as it should.

Permanent assembly may begin as soon as progressive fitting and indexing are complete. Disassemble from the top down. Lay out the parts in a clear space. Start with the bottom part. Spread the solvent on both surfaces. Press the parts together quickly. Align the index marks accurately. A little ooze-out should

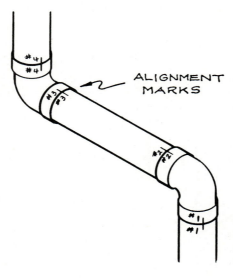

ALIGNMENT MARKS

Figure 2-5 Indexing PVC pipe is accomplished with matchup alignment lines and reference numbers.

be seen around the joint, which will assure an air- and watertight joint.

Pressure testing is required in most municipalities. This involves plugging the lines, filling them with water, and applying air pressure through a valve. The amateur home plumber may have to call in the master plumber overseer for this service, as the equipment involved is not readily available any other way.

WATER SUPPLY PIPE ASSEMBLY

Assembly of water pipes requires a different element of attention. Since these pipes are run in pairs to the sinks, tubs, and showers, it must be kept in mind that the ultimate destination calls for the cold water to come out on the right side and the hot on the left. Some manufacturers of PVC pipe make the cold pipes white in color and the hot pipes orange. This makes installation simple. In the case of copper pipe or cream-colored PVC used for both hot and cold, a system is needed to avoid crossing over and reversing lines at the destination. Several techniques can be devised. A simple foolproof method is to run all cold-water lines first. Then go back over the course and run the hot lines. Another technique is to identify the hot-water lines with a ring of black electrician's tape at the end of each pipe. A can of orange aerosol paint can be used to code a hot pipe near its end. Avoid getting paint on the end where the solvent will be used. Whatever the system used, it will be worth the effort. Retrofitting a bungled job is costly and aggravating.

Working with copper in terms of assembly and sequence is similar to working with PVC, but the tools are different. Some of the tools and supplies required are a pipe cutter, a soldering torch, steel wool, and flux. Watching a pro sweat copper pipe together makes it look easy. If one has never done it, there should be an adequate program of practice before attempting a full house job. Set up pipes and joints in various angles and positions and solder them until proficiency is gained. Put together, take apart, clean, and reassemble until confidence exists.

Hazards of plumbing with copper are present whenever an open flame is used. The dry wood of the exposed framing is particularly vulnerable. Whenever a joint is made with wood close by, a tin shield or asbestos cloth should be used to guard the wood. An adequate fire extinguisher at hand is a basic requirement.

□ DUCTWORK

Forced-air heating plants move hot air through round or rectangular sheet-metal corridors called ducts. Cold-air return ducts are not necessarily made of metal. A commonly utilized method of ducting cold air back to the furnace is to "pan" a couple of side-by-side joist cavities. Sheet metal is nailed to the underside of the joists. A register opening is cut in the floor above.

A main trunk line duct for warm-air distribution is frequently run the length of a basement or crawl space. The most efficient location is next to the girder. In this position the register "takeoff" runs will be of comparable length (Fig. 2-6). This large, rectangular duct is sometimes called a plenum trunk. Smaller ducts, most often round, elbow out of the top of the trunk and proceed down a joist cavity toward a register. The connection between this pipe and the register is called a boot (Fig. 2-7). The boot may exit through the floor or through the sole plate of the wall. The system of ducting between joists is concealable; therefore, it is favored for finished basements.

Registers may be located in the walls or the floor. A register in an exterior wall will suffer several disadvantages. The boot, and the elbow above it, will be adjacent to the sheathing on the cold side of the wall of a conventional single 2 × 4 studded wall. A significant heat loss results, as there is little or no space behind the

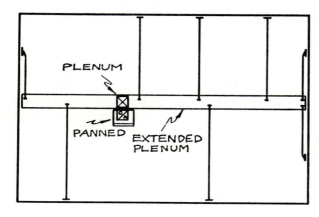

Figure 2-6 An extended plenum (trunk) with top takeoff round pipes suits the basement setup best.

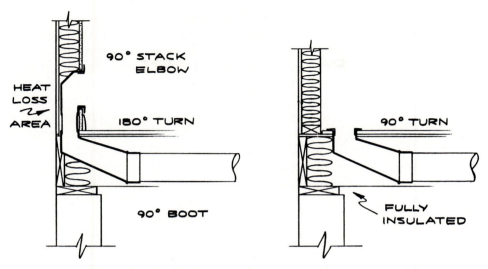

Figure 2-7 Floor outlets have advantages over wall registers during construction and after.

ductwork for adequate insulation. It is much more time consuming to cut out the sole and floor and chisel away part of the floor box header to form a rectangular opening between two studs than it is to saw a rectangle out of the floor a few inches away from the wall. Another fault of the wall register is that the heating air must do a near U turn to get into the room. Each turn reduces output velocity to a certain extent.

REGISTER LOCATION PRINCIPLES

Evolution in the building industry takes a long time. Belief in, followed by acceptance and adoption of, a principle takes even longer. The old cliché, "It was good enough for my father and his father so it's good enough for me," is frequently the stumbling block to technical progress. A case in point is the carpenter who still frames a house with a half-hatchet when there is no chopping to be done. Such a transition in the heating industry took place in the decade surrounding World War II. Central heating had been in vogue for some time. A typical installation had a large coal-burning furnace in the center of the basement. From the top rose several large, round ducts angled and spread like major limbs of a huge old tree.

In a small or moderate-sized house these asbestos-paper-covered ducts were seldom over a few feet long. Each reached into the nearest room, where a register was mounted on an interior partition. A large cold-air floor or wall register was found by the front door and sometimes another by the back door. It was a gravity-feed system where the heat rose of its own volition. The house doors, which had no weather stripping, were the greatest source of infiltration. The theory was to gather the cold air into the return register at the drafty door, as well as to pull some of the heated air from the central area across the floor. With continuously burning coal (the fire was never allowed to go out completely), the system worked fairly well. At best it was a great improvement over the European-style fireplace in each end of a house or the pot-bellied stove, where you burned on the front and froze on the rear. With the advent of natural gas and fuel oil the era of the coal-fired furnace was doomed, much to the delight of all the young lads whose duty it was to fire and maintain the furnace. Conversion units popped up all over the country. The old cast-iron grates were taken out of the firebox and an oil or gas conversion burner was shoved in through the ash dump door. The problem with the new innovation was that it did not work. The newfangled thermostat would call for heat and the flame would ignite. It had to burn a long time before the rooms warmed up. The house would heat up momentarily, but the cast-iron or firebrick firebox did not absorb or sustain the intermittent heat. As soon as the thermostat shut down the burner, the rooms would cool rapidly. Few houses had insulation of any type. Some people went back to coal. Others hung on and complained until the industry came through with electric blowers to move the hot air at a faster rate. This helped with new units but did little for the conversions, as the blowers simply removed more quickly what little warmth the firebox walls gained. Conversions were soon known universally for their inefficiency and high cost of operation.

Meanwhile, consumers with new gas or oil furnaces complained about the great temperature variation between on and off cycles and about cold spots and drafty areas. Tests showed that there could be as much as 7 to 10° difference from an interior-wall side of a room to an exterior-wall side and even more from floor to ceiling. When smoke tests were run, it was found that cold air spilled down the windows and doors and slid into the room. In the meantime the hot air from the traditional centrally located registers was going directly to the ceiling.

    Perimeter heating was not born in the twentieth century. When U.S. troops went into Korea in the early 1950s, they witnessed perimeter heating as it has been practiced in parts of the Orient for centuries. Clay pipes laid around a one-room dwelling had several exit holes into the room at various places around the perimeter. A small fire was built adjacent to a larger hole. A person would be stationed there operating a hand bellows to push warm air from the fire into and around the pipe.

    In an effort to overcome the many problems encountered during the evolution from hard fuel to liquid fuel and gas, heating engineers reversed the register location, putting hot registers under windows and cold return(s) in a central interior location. The success was remarkable.

    It is now the standard of the industry for hot-air registers to be placed under windows and adjacent to doors. The hot air warms the entering cold air. As it moves toward centrally located cold-air returns, it is tempered. Very little temperature variation exists throughout the room.

LOW REGISTERS VERSUS HIGH REGISTERS

The controversy continues about the location of registers in slab-floor houses. It seems to be all too common for some builders to rationalize a system as adequate when it is easier or less costly to install. Some technicians and engineers will concoct elaborate quasi-documentation to (seemingly) prove a system. Such has been the case for furnaces and ductwork placed in the attic with registers in the ceiling or high on a wall. The real reason for using this inefficient location is more apt to be a reluctance to get involved in underslab duct planning, preparation, and placement. Another reason is the loss of space taken up by a furnace on the slab. Only one test will really prove the superiority of the floor register compared to attic installations. That is to have two identical houses to field test, each with a different system. To date there appears to be no documentation of such a practical test to validate a ceiling installation. Where comfort and minimum operational cost are the criteria, the homebuilder will be wise to place the heat entrances at floor level and by the perimeter walls. Heat rises naturally. It is difficult or at least more costly to force it down from high registers. The ducts under a slab or crawl space may fan out wagonwheel fashion (Fig. 2-8) directly from the hub (the heat plenum exchanger). Disproportionately long runs can be accommodated with larger-diameter pipes.

The furnace on a slab will be a reverse-flow type called a counterflow. The hot air is discharged out the bottom, and the used air returns through the top. A lowered ceiling in a centrally located corridor serves well as a return-air duct conveyer. Registers face into rooms that are adjacent.

Duct-size proportioning in a crawl space or basement needs to be determined quite carefully lest the plenum trunk be turned into a pressurized manifold or the rooms be pressurized. A trunk that is too large for the quantity of air taken off by the duct runs will cause the blower to overwork. The number of square inches of air taken off the trunk determines the trunk cross-section size. It should match closely. For example, if there are to be eight registers in a house and the furnace is centrally located there might be four feeder ducts from a trunk on each side of the furnace. If the feeder ducts are 6″ in diameter, there is a total of 170 square inches to be supplied, 85 square inches toward each half. A trunk line with a cross section dimension of 8″ × 12″ (96 square inches) would supply adequate air down each side. If the furnace is placed at the end of this house and uses a single trunk, it would have to start out being 8″ × 24″ (Fig. 2-9). The size could be funneled down after it passed a takeoff, or two, or more. Let us say that it is reduced once at a point after four runs have been taken off. The trunk plenum would start out with a size of 8″ × 24″ and reduce to 8″ × 12″.

A limiting and controlling gauge at the time of planning will be the size of the hot-air opening on the furnace. The total cross

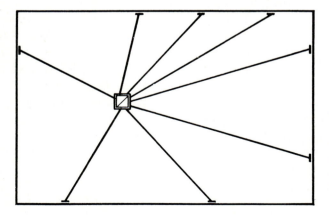

Figure 2-8 A box plenum on the bottom of this counterflow furnace with individual round pipes adapts well to crawl spaces and slab floors. Cold air is drawn through wall registers into the top.

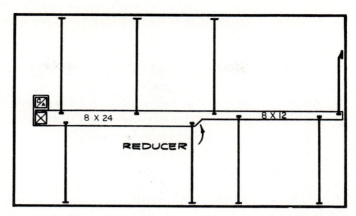

Figure 2-9 A plenum trunk may be reduced in size proportionately according to what percentage of the load remains.

section of the trunk lines should not exceed the square-inch size of the opening through which the air must pass coming out of the furnace. The opening is designed to accommodate the capacity of the fan to move air.

CENTRAL VACUUM

A central vacuum-cleaning system is relatively simple to install. There is a semipermanent location to be established for the collector tank. A spot in the basement or in an attached garage is preferred over one in the house. From the tank a permanently installed rigid tube will extend through the house. These pipes are generally made of lightweight PVC. They are assembled to elbows and Ts with the same technique as that used for water drains and vents. The room outlet covers have plunger switches so that when the cover is lifted the vacuum motor on the remote tank turns on.

Locating vacuum outlets follows the philosophy that all corners and the interior of the house should be reachable by the flexible hose that plugs into an outlet. Therefore, if a 20′ hose is supplied for a rectangular house that is 28′ wide and 56′ long, two outlets on a centrally located bearing wall could serve a minimum requirement. Careful assessment of the floor plan may reveal that three or more well-spaced outlets would be a wiser choice. From an operational standpoint, the system will work better with fewer outlets, as there is less leakage from covers as the gaskets deteriorate.

Because the system works on an airtight suction principle, each cemented joint must be airtight. Unlike a poor water connection, which leaks out, the vacuum leak will suck air into the pipe. After the piping has been assembled and cemented, it should be tested. With all outlet covers closed, jump the switch wire at any outlet, which will turn on the motor. Use a smoke tester or water around the outside of every joint that has been made. If there is a leak, the smoke or water will be drawn into the pipe through the hole. Such a pinhole leak can usually be sealed by applying solvent directly over the leak while the motor is running. The suction draws the solvent in and simultaneously dries it.

Caution: Do not allow the vacuum motor to run longer than enough to check a joint or two at one location. Because there is no vacuum outlet open, the suction fan is drawing against a "dead head," which may cause it to burn out the motor.

☐ WIRING

Wiring is the most adaptable of the three utility conveyers. It can easily be routed around rigid pipes, ducts, and structural materials. Therefore, it comes next to last in the sequence of concealed installations.

To assure safety, electric components that are a permanent part of a structure are highly regulated by local and national codes. Inadequate wiring can lead to overloading a line (more demand is put on a circuit than the wires can carry). In such a case, the excess heat generated will "blow" (melt) a fuse or trip a breaker. Fuses and breakers are matched to wire size. Putting a penny under a fuse should never be done, nor should a larger fuse be installed than the wire size indicates. Such practices only nullify the safety reasons for having a fuse or breaker. These safety devices are there to warn of a problem and to prevent a sustained overload that might result in fire.

WIRE SIZE AND LOAD

Understanding the relationship of wire size to demand on it is important for a house builder, whether the builder does the work or contracts out the wiring job. There is a layman's formula with which to compute the size of wire needed for a particular circuit. A *circuit* is a leg of the system composed of so many feet of wire and so many outlets and fixtures that will be safeguarded by one safety breaker in the main panel box. Wire is code numbered according to the amperage it will carry. In theory, 1 amp will carry 100 watts of load. To find out how many watts of load a wire size will carry, apply the following formula: amps × volts = watts (A × V = W).

Houses built in the period between World War I and World War II made use of electricity primarily for lighting. An average-size house of one or two stories commonly had a 60-amp fuse box containing four circuits of 15-amp capacity each. The wire size was number 14. At 110 volts, this netted a theoretical circuit capacity of 1650 watts or, at 115 volts, 1725 watts.

As more and more electrical gadgets and appliances became popular and available, it became mandatory to include greater capacity in the electrical system. By the end of World War II, the average new house was sporting a 100-amp system. Today it is common to find entrance panels with a capacity for 20 or 30 circuit breakers with amperage capacities of 150 or 200. The National Electric Code is constantly being updated with new and more demanding requirements. The certified electrician must keep informed and be abreast of the latest demands.

The wire size in standard use today is number 12 with ground. The cable will contain two insulated wires (white and black) and a bare ground wire. The number 12 wire is rated at 20 amps. In theory, this size should carry 2200 watts at 110 volts up to 2400 watts at 120 volts. In practice, a load is planned for not more than 75 percent of capacity. This yields a 25 percent margin of safety, which guards against an unknowledgeable person who plugs in several cords to a particular duplex outlet and unwittingly chances an overload.

Unique loads may require a separate circuit alone. Examples are a furnace, a water heater, a dishwasher, the kitchen range, a garbage disposal, and a trash compactor. Amperage, wire, and breaker size must be sized correctly for each appliance.

Self-wiring is permitted in most regions of the United States by the homeowner house builder provided that all codes are met or exceeded and the job passes inspection. Some municipalities require that the installer do the job under the license umbrella of a certified (licensed) electrician. In any case, the job is within the scope of the budget-minded builder. It requires study and comprehension of a good text with understandable diagrams and adherence to the code.

INSTALLATION TECHNIQUES

Some helpful hints may avoid some sour notes later in the job. Two difficult and frustrating troubleshooting experiences stand out in the author's experience. The house was near completion. Interior plastered walls were being painted. It was difficult to get enough light to see the depth of color in the bathroom for a second coat, so the painter rigged a floodlight. Then he switched on the mirror lights. They grew dim and went out. A check of the breaker revealed that it had tripped. Since the light had been tested before covering the walls and turned on many times since, a real mystery existed. A new breaker did not change anything. The wiring plan was consulted, which revealed that an adjacent bedroom was on the same circuit. The painting was taking place in the evening. The lights were also on in the bedroom. A 6′ long baseboard hot-water heat convector had been nailed to the wall between a pair of duplex outlets. Touching one of the bare nailheads that held the convector to the wall brought a tiny tingle to the fingers. A check of the metal surface with a voltage tester indicated some "juice" in the metal. One by one the nails that held the convector were pulled. The third nail pulled was an 8d common. The voltmeter went dead. There was the culprit. A small hole was cut in the plaster to reveal the cause of the short. The nail had penetrated the hole in the stud through which the electric wire went from one duplex to the next and then on to the bathroom. The nail had passed between the two wires in the cable, touching neither directly. It skinned enough of the insulation from each individual wire to cause a minute leakage across. When all the lights were on and the extra flood added, it was enough to overload the bleeding circuit and cause the voltage drop farther down the line in the bathroom.

This story points up the logic for drilling wire passage holes in the studs as nearly centered as possible so that nails through the exterior sheathing will not be hit by the auger bit nor will plasterboard nails on the interior of the wall enter the cable holes. Obviously, nails that are long enough to enter a hole that is centered in the 3½" width of a stud should not be used in the known vicinity of wiring.

Another case of bleeding current was found at a knockout hole in the entrance box. An overzealous electrician's trainee had tightened down much too hard on a wire clamp. The clamp squashed the cable insulation just enough to cause a bleeding short across the wire, but not enough to trip the breaker until an additional load was placed on the circuit. Clamps that squeeze vinyl insulation should never be cinched more than snugly.

The same is true of staples. Very slight contact of the staple with the wire is all that is required. Do not drive a staple over a wire to an extent that the wire covering is pressed. Pulling a staple should never be done by prying out with a screwdriver or hammer claws. Use nothing between the staple and the cable, as the insulation will surely be squashed. Pull staples only from the outer side with pliers. Grasp the staple squarely across the top and pull straight up.

STRINGING WIRE

Some professionals will take pride in the appearance of the wire after it is strung. An effort will be made to avoid spiraling the wire as it is pulled through holes in the structural wood members. The wire is drawn from the center of a coil through a cutout hole in the cardboard packing box. To avoid spiraling, the wire box will have to be revolved many times to counteract the spiraling. Not much concern is given this problem in walls. It becomes more noticeable in basements where wiring is frequently left exposed.

Parallel or diagonal stringing is another option open to the person stringing wires. Again the location may be the element of determination. Exposed wiring in a basement is usually run parallel or at a 90° angle to the joists. Coming out of the entrance box the several cables are run in neat, parallel formation up the wall to a joist cavity. Passing along the joist channels, the wires are stapled to the face of the joist. When a turning point is reached, a gentle curve is made with the cable. From that point on it is necessary to drill a hole through each joist through which to pass the cable. Several cables may be run through the same hole. A ½" hole is the minimum size for a single cable; however, a ⅝" hole will make the pulling easier. Larger holes are needed as more cables are run together.

Hole location should be in the upper third of the joist whenever possible to get a drill into position. Go no closer than 2″ to the deck sheathing lest the auger hit a hidden nail from the floor sheathing. Keep the hole or holes close to the outer or inner bearing ends of the joint so that any potential weakening will be held to a minimum.

Diagonal stringing of wires is sometimes practiced under two conditions. Where the wire is under the floor in a crawl space, the appearance is not a consideration. A wire may be taken in a straight line from its origin to its destination. If one wishes to make the route quite straight, a chalk line is snapped on the underside of the joists. The marks left by the chalk will indicate the angle that the hole is drilled. Since the shortest distance between two points is a straight line, it follows that a considerable amount of wire footage can be saved by this method.

Hanging wires from bare staples on the underedge of joists is a poor practice. In time, floor vibration and the weight of the wire can cause wire insulation to fail. In turn, a voltage leak across the staple may develop. In damp crawl spaces the staples may rust enough to disintegrate completely over a period of years.

Wiring in the attic may involve both parallel and diagonal systems. There will be situations where a long circuit supply wire will go straight down the attic, perhaps snuggled up to a strong back or cradled in the V of W truss webs to a junction box. From the covered steel junction box, the legs of the circuit will fan out, heading directly toward their outlets (ceiling lights, for example).

Wiring through insulation is an element to consider in the attic. Before the energy crunch of the early 1980s, many houses contained no more than 6″ of insulation between the ceiling joists. The wires could be strung and stapled over the top of the joists. This posed no great problem to the insulation installer who hung the insulation from below. With present-day depths of 10 to 12″ of blanket or blown insulation, it is advisable to put as much of the wire as possible above the insulation level. It can be effectively attached to truss webs, purlins, or rafters around the perimeter.

Fixture boxes are positioned slightly above the finished ceiling level. In this position the light-fixture cover will pull up tightly to the ceiling when the screws are installed into the box.

A simple gauge to check box position (distance below the ceiling joists) can be made from a scrap of ½" plywood about 8 to 10" wide and 30" long (Fig. 2-10). Cut out two or three holes just large enough to encompass an octagon metal fixture box or a round plastic box. Ceiling joists will be spaced on centers 16" or 24" apart. Box location frequently falls between them. The gauge board is held tightly on the underside spanning two joists, with one of the test holes over the box. No part of the box should protrude below the board for a ceiling made of ½" gypsum board.

Locating a fixture in the center of a rectangular room is a simple task. Set a temporary nail in the junction of each corner at the ceiling level. String a diagonal line between the two nails in opposite corners. Without cutting the line, take it across the wall, either right or left, wind it around the third nail, and string it diagonally across the room to the remaining unoccupied nail. The intersection of the string indicates the center of the room. Center the box directly over the string intersection.

Two or more fixtures should be located in the approximate center of each half of a long, rectangular room (Fig. 2-11). Dividing

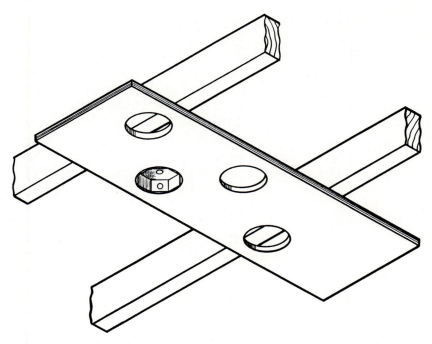

Figure 2-10 This gauge board may be used to check the correct electric box depth below the ceiling joists.

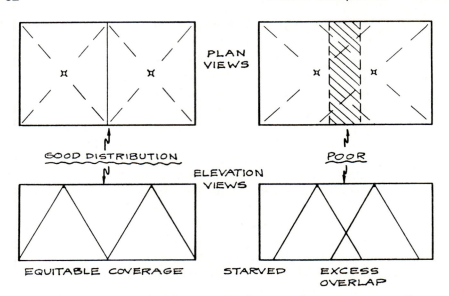

Figure 2-11 Ceiling fixture placed in equal room segments disperses the light more equitably.

the length of a room into thirds for the placement of two lights might seem logical from an appearance point of view; however, the distribution of light will be unequal. Dividing a room in thirds, especially one with dark-paneled walls, will cause the center of the room to be brighter where the light beams overlap. The ends of the room will be dimmer. A room whose walls are painted white or a very light color will reflect the light back into the room better. Even so, there will be a concentrated area between the two lights where too much overlap occurs. Fixture placement with light walls is less critical. For a room that is less than twice as long as wide, the placement of two lights will be an educated estimate based on the factor of lighting overlap between the fixtures and the reflective potential of the wall coloring. The distribution of light will usually be better where there is more space between the lights than between a light and an adjacent wall.

DOORBELLS, CHIMES, AND THERMOSTATS

Wiring to signal devices such as doorbells and chimes and wires to thermostats are usually of the low-voltage type. A transformer is placed at a conveniently exposed location so that it can be replaced readily should it wear out and fail. Power for a single bell can be taken from the closest power source to the bell or to its button. The transformer is positioned between the 110-volt source and the bell or button. A chime with a button at the front and rear doors will require more forethought in choosing the best power source and the placement of the transformer and the wires. Sometimes, where multiple annunciators exist, the transformer will be mounted in the entrance breaker box. Keep in mind that low-voltage bell wire is much less costly than number 14 or 12 wire.

Bells and chimes should be located in accordance with their intended function. A chime with a single tone for the service entrance and a double tone to indicate that someone is at the main entrance must be located in a position that can be heard from all rooms in the house.

Chimes may be recessed in the wall for two reasons. A créche-type recess (arched top) has been popular for many years. Aside from the enhanced beauty of long brass tubes hanging in a recess, there is a practical reason. Frequently, the chime is located in a corridor, a traffic area. Protruding from the wall surface, the chime could be a hazard. A recess permits the entire mechanism to be out of harm's way.

All or a portion of the back of the recess must have a wooden backup plate to anchor the screws from which the chime box will hang (Fig. 2-12). This wood backer is handily made from ½ or ⅝" sheathing plywood sandwiched between the wallboard on the other side of the wall and the piece that forms the back of the recess.

The thermostat that controls the heating and cooling temperature of the entire house must be located with great care. The thermostat must be in a spot where the sun will never shine on it, summer or winter. It should be centrally located on an interior partition. It must not be in the direct line of a hot-air register, nor should it be above a cold-air return. Avoid a location that would expose the thermostat to the heat of an electric lamp or a fireplace. To produce the best blend of temperature between the floor and ceiling, locate the thermostat midway up the wall.

Thermostat wire may be run through the stud wall to the furnace, or it may be routed up into the attic or down into the crawl space or basement. Whichever route is most conserving of wire may be the basis of choice. On the other hand, a route that provides the least amount of drilling may be compelling.

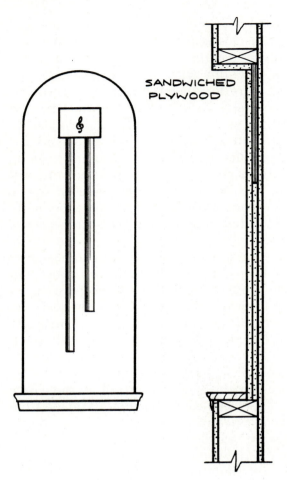

SANDWICHED
PLYWOOD

Figure 2-12 A recess, such as one for a door chime, should be backed with wood.

TELEPHONE AND CABLE TV

These wiring jobs are usually carried out by company personnel, at no cost in some cities. This being the case, it only becomes necessary to place your order for a convenient time. That time is before any wall covering has been put on the interior of the framework. It is best to have the electrical wiring service completed before the telephone or TV wiring is started. It will prevent conflicts of outlet location. The TV installer, particularly, can coordinate the antenna outlets better with the electrical duplex outlets into which a television set will most likely be plugged.

6 CABINET SOFFITS

Upper built-in cabinets in the kitchen and sometimes those in a bathroom will have boxed-out areas above the cabinets called soffits. Sometimes this closed dummy boxing is called a bulkhead because its construction is similar to that of the compartmented areas in large ships. The purpose of the cabinet soffit is simply to close in a more or less inaccessible area so that it does not become a dust catcher. Most homemakers who are principal occupants of the kitchen cannot reach the area of the soffit, so it is considered a nonfunctional place by the majority of builders.

The standard height of the soffit is 12″. There is a potential of several cubic feet of storage in the soffit location for those brave souls who do not fear mounting a step stool. The author has utilized this area in several houses to add a cubic foot of storage for each linear foot of counter and appliance frontage simply by installing 1′ high cabinets above the regular cabinets.

SOFFIT CONSTRUCTION

The framework of a soffit is attached directly to the wall studs and the ceiling joists; therefore, it is constructed before the walls are covered. There are many different ways to "hang" a soffit successfully. Only a few examples are shown and described on these pages. Should one deviate from these plans, it will be prudent to keep one principle in mind. All members that support the weight of the soffit by hanging from the rafters should be attached with nails at angles to take advantage of the principle of shear stress (not tension), lest the weight pull the soffit down from the ceiling.

Parallel soffits are those that run in the same direction as the ceiling joists. Intersecting soffits are those that cross the ceiling joist, usually at right angles. Hanging the crossing soffit is less complicated, as there is a ceiling joist every 16″ or 24″ from which a hanger board may be attached.

Two basic methods of construction stand out for the builder's choice. One uses the structural-framework principle. The other uses the box-beam principle. The structural-framework technique may be less costly if it can be done by using scraps of 2 × 4s that might otherwise be discarded. The box-beam technique is quicker to build but may cost more for materials. Where there is a high labor cost factor, the box-beam method could cost less.

A structural framework soffit (Fig. 2-13) is started by building a facia frame. The work is done on the floor. A 2 × 4 forms the top of this ladderlike structure, and another 2 × 4 of identical length forms the bottom leading edge of the soffit facia. When in position, both pieces will have their flat surfaces on a horizontal plane.

Hold or temporarily tack the top 2 × 4 to the ceiling joists. Mark lines across the top of the board along both sides of each joist. The vertical cripple studs forming the facia ladder will all be placed to the right or to the left of these marks with their edges on the line. Lower the board to the floor. Remove the nails. Lay the board alongside the other 2 × 4 and transfer the stud locations to the second board.

The soffit height is 12″ in a room that has been framed with precut studs. The underside of the soffit should be at or near a height of 7′ above the floor. In taller rooms the soffit will be higher,

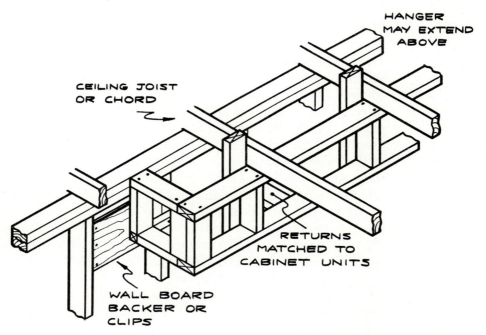

HANGER MAY EXTEND ABOVE

CEILING JOIST OR CHORD

RETURNS MATCHED TO CABINET UNITS

WALL BOARD BACKER OR CLIPS

Figure 2-13 A soffit may be preassembled on the floor, hoisted into place, and attached to the ceiling joists and wall studs.

to make up the difference. In the standard-height room, the cripple studs in the facia frame will be duplicate cut to a length of 9″. The 2 × 4s on the top and bottom add 3″ to net a 12″ high frame. Nail the frame together the same as on a stud wall using the angled-nail pincher technique. Note in Fig. 2-13 that the end stud is faced differently where a soffit ends in the open (not against a wall). This covering system permits the corner to be secured together with top and bottom nails instead of toenails.

Hanger boards are installed next. This board is a 2 × 4 that will extend from the bottom edge of the soffit to the top of the ceiling joist or a few inches above. Its minimum length will be 12″ plus the joist height (3½, 5½, or 7¼″). Where blown insulation is specified, it will be advantageous to allow a few inches to protrude above the joist. This will help eliminate the possibility of the upper end of the hanger splitting when it is nailed to the joist. Where a double layer of insulation blanket is to be used, the second layer will run across the joists. In this case the protruding hangers are objectionable as they protrude into the second layer of insulation. The hangers should be cut to fit flush with the top of the joists.

Nail a hanger to the back side of the facia over each cripple stud where ceiling joists or chords are on 2′ centers. A hanger nailed to every other joist may be adequate where joists are on 16″ centers. Place two 16d sinkers or box nails into the top board, one nail in the center of the cripple, and two nails into the bottom board. Tap holes must be bored for the two bottom holes. Even if it were possible to nail this location without splitting, the board will probably split later from the heat and shrinkage. The top of the cabinets are anchored to the lower 2 × 4, which is hanging from these nailed straps. Splits from the nails at the bottom of a hanger strap will render it less than adequately supportive.

The bottom ladder may be assembled to the facia ladder on the floor or it may be stick built to the facia and wall after the facia is hung. Retro assembly will virtually make the cripple installation a 100 percent toenailing job. If this is to be avoided, the back board against the wall can be nailed to the cripples before hoisting into place. End nailing of these cripples is superior to toenailing. However, the other end of the cripples will be toenailed to the bottom facia 2 × 4 since it is impractical to nail through the 3½″ width of the board.

Placement of cripple studs is sometimes coordinated with the cabinet modules so that screws can be placed into them at the end of each cabinet top frame. It is difficult to accomplish this objective precisely, so it is more often ignored than practiced. Cripples in the soffit bottom should be omitted from the area where an electrical box is specified. Cripple location will not be critical where an external fluorescent fixture is used. A wire pigtail is left hanging through a hole in the wall covering. It is attached inside the fluorescent box later. Spacing of the cripples is not crucial. There should be one at the ends of all soffits and others to serve as spanners about every 16″ or less.

The depth of the soffit is not a standardized figure. It depends somewhat on whether there will be a molding around the top of the cabinet and how big it is. In the United States, the cabinet itself is quite standardized at 12″. On the soffit the added thickness of wall covering (wallboard, paneling, or whatever) can be ignored if the same thickness of material is put on the wall below the soffit. Therefore, if a ¾″ cove molding is to be used, the soffit should extend a minimum of 1″ beyond the cabinet. This will permit a ¼″ overhang of the soffit beyond the molding, provided all components are perfectly straight. Since this is seldom the case with wood, most builders will opt for a greater overhang in order to get the parallel comparison of the molding at a greater distance from the edge of the soffit. A 13″ depth is an absolute minimum; 14″ would not be considered excessive. Wider moldings will call for even more horizontal depth.

The lower back board can be made of a half of a 2 × 4 (2 × 2). It will be positioned with its greatest width vertical so that a uniform 1½″ faces into the room. Half a 2 × 4 measures approximately 1¹¹⁄₁₆″ × 1½″. The sawed edge is faced up. A 14″-deep soffit design will take horizontal cripples 9″ in length, the same as the verticals, so they can be duplicate cut together with the vertical cripples. Their summation is: lower front board, 3½″, plus cripple, 9″, plus back board, 1½″, equals 14″.

Raising the soffit is at least a two-person job. Assuming that the entire soffit has been assembled on the floor, there still remain some details of alignment to be done first. Measure out from the top plate the exact distance of the horizontal depth of the soffit frame where the soffit starts and where it ends. Snap a chalk line along the underside of the ceiling joists. Measure down the studs at each end of the soffit location from the joists the exact height of the soffit frame. Strike a chalk line between these points. Hoist the soffit frame into position. Wedge it up at the ends with a couple of braces to the floor. Nail through the hanger boards that are closest to the ends. Use only one nail at this point. Slant each nail downward to give shear support. Push the facia in or pull it out until it lines up with the chalk line. Nail a hanger adjacent to the center of the soffit. While pushing in or out, nail all the other hangers. Put only one nail in at the top of each hanger, as the lower part of the soffit may need to be pulled in or pushed out, in which case the hangers will need to pivot slightly. Attach a string line across the front edge of the bottom board of the soffit. Pull it very tight and position it about a nail diameter below the front edge. Start a few nails into the back board. Line up the ends first about 1/16″ higher than the chalk line on the studs. Having the back board slightly high will cause the front edge of the cabinet to snug up tightly to the soffit. Set the nails at the ends. Set one at the center after aligning the board above the line. Now check the front lower string line. If the front edge is behind the line, the back board will need shimming out. If the front board cannot be pushed back to the line, locate the stud or studs that are protruding and notch them until the board in front lines up perfectly. Permanently set all the nails in the back board.

Check the horizontal straightness of the front lower edge next. Even though a single nail is set in each hanger, it will move a little if need be. It is important that this edge at the front be as straight as possible as it is the most visible. Tap the hangers up or down to make the edge perfectly straight, in accordance with the string. Remember, the string must be very taut to give a true no-sag reference.

Bar clamps are very useful to the soffit installer. Two 24″ clamps will make it possible for one person to adjust and complete the nailing of the soffit. Bar clamps have a nasty habit of falling off once pounding begins. If a pair of clamps is all that is supporting the soffit before nailing begins, it will be prudent to block the clamp in position with a 16d nail or a loop of wire around the bar and a joist.

Backup plates are needed at or behind the ends of the soffit. These two areas present a vulnerable spot for a crack to develop in plaster or gypsum board. The backerboard is made and installed the same as curtain and fixture backers. The backer is easier to install before the soffit goes up; however, it is possible to retrofit them in most situations.

Insulating the soffit makes sense, as there is no reason to heat or cool a nonfunctional dead space. The wall behind the soffit should be insulated before the soffit is installed. As the ceiling will have fill insulation or blown-in cellulose, it is an easy matter to fill the soffits simultaneously. It is more time consuming to cut and fit blanket or batt insulation into the soffit, but it will be worth it over a period of years. The latter will be done from the room side after all electrical wiring, hood vents, and any other hidden installations have been placed.

PARALLEL SOFFITS

L-shaped and U-shaped kitchens will have one of the two or three soffit legs running parallel to the ceiling joists. This necessitates a different support arrangement, as there is rarely a joist in a perfectly aligned position for hangers to be attached. However, it is usually possible to use the ceiling backer board blocks that secure the partition as an anchoring board for the soffit hanger (Fig. 2-14). A U-shaped kitchen has partitions around the U. Whichever

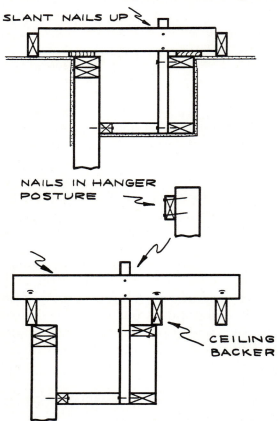

SLANT NAILS UP

NAILS IN HANGER POSTURE

CEILING BACKER

Figure 2-14 A parallel soffit may be effectively hung from the cross blocks above the ceiling backup board or from purlins crossing the two joists between which the soffit is located.

wall(s) runs parallel to the soffit will have ceiling nail backers and blocks above. The soffit hangers and cripples must be calculated carefully to coincide with the location of the overhead backer blocks.

BOXED SOFFITS

A boxed soffit uses surface plywood as a part of its structural integrity. The frame on which the plywood is nailed may be simplified, built with fewer hangers and spanners (cripples), because the plywood forms a continuous backing for its finish covering (Fig. 2-15). The stiffness and no-sag characteristic of plywood on edge makes it possible to have fewer hangers to support its length. A hanger every 4' or less will usually be adequate. An 8'-long, free-standing soffit (unattached to walls at one or both ends) can be hung from a hanger in the center and one from each end. The wall-butting end of a soffit requires no hanger, as it will be nailed through its frame into a backer board on the wall.

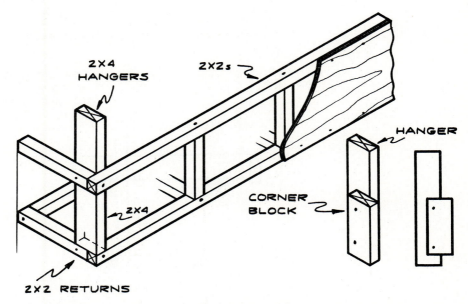

Figure 2-15 A plywood-sheathed soffit gains strength and rigidity from the boxing principle. Structural members can therefore be smaller and hangers fewer in number.

A soffit over 8′ long will take more than one piece of plywood. Wherever the butt joint of the plywood is made, a hanger should be placed. Therefore, a cripple and hanger must be correlated with the ceiling joist above, and the plywood joint made over the center of the cripple.

Another feature to remember with the plywood-boxed soffit is to reduce the size of the cross-section frame girth by the thickness of the plywood sheathing, since the thickness of the wall covering is yet to be included (Fig. 2-16). For example, the frame without boxing is to be 12″ high. Therefore, a frame to be boxed with ½″ plywood should be 11½″ high.

Also remember to form solid corners at the free-standing end of a soffit. It makes no difference which piece of sheathing runs past the corner, the end piece or the facia piece. One is cut flush

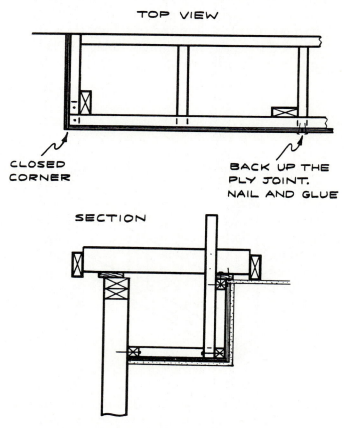

Figure 2-16   Details of a boxed soffit.

with the framework corner. The other fully laps the end of the first piece to form a solid corner.

A soffit usually continues uninterrupted over windows, range hoods, refrigerators, and built-in ovens. It is good to know in advance where vents from these appliances will, of necessity, pass through into the attic. By having this information, it will be possible to avoid cutting out ("butchering") structural members. Also, one can provide structural backup from which to mount a hood or light fixture.

7 INSULATING THE WALLS AND CEILING

After all the framework is completed and all the hidden wires, pipes, and recesses have been installed in the exterior walls, it will be time to install the insulation. Two considerations are important at the outset. One deals with the quantity of insulation to be used. The other relates to the quality of the installation process. Both need to be examined due to the long-range implications on operational economy.

Quantity concepts changed drastically in the early 1980s. "Thermal" construction became the magical word with which to clinch a new house sale. Unfortunately, many houses masquerading as "thermal" were only moderately well insulated. Many window brands with two glass panes set in butyl are characterized as thermal although the advantage is scarcely different from that of single panes with storm windows. The term "thermal" is so broad that it can be used to describe any form or quantity of added material that resists the passage of heat. A consumer can easily be a victim of the residual of the barest minimum of insulation described as thermal or the benefactor of a truly well conceived and insulated house. Only when he or she knows the precise quantity and type of insulation material used and the quality of the application will it be possible to predict the comfort and the cost of living in a particular house.

The quality of installations, one might think, would be fairly uniform in the construction industry. It is not. There is a great potential for losing the optimum insulation capability of insulation by poor installation. A 3½″ batt of insulation placed between studs, for example, in theory will provide a resistance factor of 11 (R-11). In actual practice, this will occur only when the blanket is perfectly installed. Faulty installation is characterized by several things. A gap at the top or around an electrical outlet box will be detrimental. Any place where the fibers are unduly compressed, kinked, lapped, or not permitted to expand fully into the opening will subtract from the full potential. For maximum efficiency, all surfaces and edges of blanket-type insulation must be in contact with the surrounding woodwork and sheathing.

QUANTITY OF INSULATION

Countrywide zoning maps are available from various sources that indicate the recommended quantity of insulation and/or the minimum R value for any area of the United States. Utility companies, municipal building inspection offices, and insulation manufacturers are ready sources of this information. Generally, R-19 is being specified for walls in all but the extreme southern belt. R-11 used to be an accepted standard until fuel cost began to skyrocket in the late 1970s and early 1980s.

The R-11 batt or blanket is customized to coincide with the 3½″ depth of a stud. Therefore, a 2 × 4 stud wall cavity is limited to R-11 in the core. It is possible and practical to raise the resistance factor by sheathing the outer walls with a high-intensity insulation board in order to approach the R-19 goal. Dense Styrofoam and beadboard sheet materials will be advantageous for this purpose. A close scrutiny and some adaptation will be required to make up for the lost holding power of siding nails, as the foam boards have no holding power whatever. Similarly, other methods and materials will be required to achieve adequate windbracing objectives.

The 6″ stud wall was conceived in the northern United States specifically for its superior depth to accommodate 6″ of blanket insulation (R-19). In conjunction with sheet-type insulboards of high R rating, a superior thermal wall can be achieved. To gain an alternative cost-comparable design, one has but to consider the double-wall design. It will prove more than 25 percent superior to a 6″ wall with comparable sheathing.

Ceiling insulation is equally or more critical in terms of quantity and installation. Because heat rises it will collect under the ceiling and ultimately escape through the materials. A general rule of thumb is that the insulation in a ceiling should rate about twice as high as the wall up to R-40. From there on, the diminishing cost-effectiveness warrants consideration.

There are three generally accepted forms of insulation for ceilings: blanket, blown, and fill. Blanket is the expanded glass-fiber type, which comes in rolls and in two widths, to fit 16 or 24" spaced ceiling joists. It can be purchased with a paper-backing vapor barrier or "unfaced." Blown insulation is a form of fire-retardant-treated cellulose. It gets its name from the technique of blowing it into an attic with air pressure. Fill insulation is a loose bead or granular-type insulation that is simply emptied from bags into the attic and spread to a uniform depth. Some of the materials commonly available are perlite, vermiculite, and Zonalite. Although the fill insulations are relatively easy to install, they suffer from a serious fault unless used in a confined space. In a typical attic that is adequately ventilated, the wind currents will shift the lightweight fill from one area to another, thus destroying the uniformity of depth that is desirable.

ATTIC INSULATION

Blanket insulation may be laid in a single layer to the same depth as the ceiling joists. By present standards this is seldom enough, since residential trusses usually have 2 × 4 lower chords, and conventional roofed houses seldom have ceiling joists over 2 × 6 or 2 × 8 size.

A recommended technique to attain a higher R factor is to layer the blanket insulation (Fig. 2-17). For example, should the specs call for 10" of blanket insulation, the first layer would be a 3½" blanket laid between 2 × 4 ceiling joists topped by a nominal 6" layer laid at right angles over the joists. For a 2 × 6 ceiling joist, the order would be reversed. For an R-38 requirement, two layers of 6" insulation are installed. One layer of 12" blanket laid in the joist cavities does not meet R-38, as the joists will be exposed between the blankets, permitting as much as a 20 to 50 percent loss of efficiency. This loss can be overcome by filling the channels with granulated cellulose.

Another area of great heat loss is the area directly above the exterior wall plate. Unless preplanning has netted a raised thermal truss, this area will be shallow in depth. Remember that

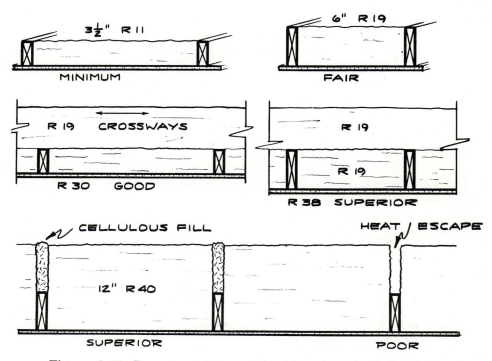

Figure 2-17   R means resistance to heat loss. Layering helps eliminate exfiltration places. Top layers are laid perpendicular to joists, bottom layers between joists.

fibrous insulations do not work well when compressed. Only when expanded are the cells large enough to encapsulate (trap) dead air and form an adequate thermal barrier. A conventional 2 × 6 rafter with a birdsmouth seat cut or a truss with 2 × 4 chords will have only about 4″ of depth from the top plate to the underside of the roof sheathing, not enough room for adequate insulation needs. This area in the ceiling is most vulnerable to heat loss by exfiltration.

   Blanket insulation is best put in before any ceiling covering, such as gypsum board, is installed. It can be installed effectively from below the ceiling only if the blankets are paper backed. The double-layering system can be all accomplished from below. This is advantageous with low-pitched roofs of 4 in 12 or less. The top layer is installed first, perpendicular to the joists (Fig. 2-18). Short pieces are cut to go over the top plates between the rafters. These pieces are made long enough so that the inner end will touch the

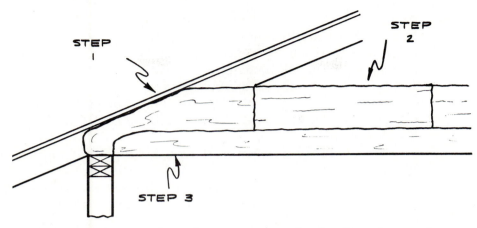

Figure 2-18 A nonthermal truss or conventional rafter setup requires special attention to avoid great heat loss over the top plates. Where there are eave vents, corridors must be arranged over the insulation.

edge of the first continuous blanket that is rolled out across the joists close to the top plate. Roll out the blanket to its full length; then slide it up against the short pieces all along the wall (Figure 2-19). Each adjacent piece to come is fluffed out and snuggled up

Figure 2-19 Insulation stops are needed when blown-in-type insulation is used or a raised truss exists.

tight to the preceding piece so that there are no air gaps. Work from each side of the roof toward the center of the ceiling. The last opening will seldom, if ever, be the exact width of the insulation, so a cut-down strip will be required. Custom fit it. Cut it a little wide so that it will compress against each side. Do not fold an overly wide piece in an attempt to make it fit. Sometimes a couple of inches of needed space can be gained by compressing the previous layers toward the eaves.

Wear safety glasses of the goggle type that hug the face. Wear a long-sleeved shirt and lightweight leather or rubber gloves. The second that you pick up the insulation, tiny particles of fiberglass begin to float about. All persons should wear a respirator mask. Persons who choose not to wear protective clothing or gloves can avoid minute slivers in the fingers to some extent by blowing across the hands after each contact with the raw fiberglass. If some irritation is experienced, it is not long lived, as simple washing will usually carry away the slivers. One should be very wary of rubbing the eyes at all times. In any case, the itching that may attend insulating is seldom significant enough that it should discourage the do-it-yourselfer.

Lay the insulation roll on the floor with the fiber side facing up and the open end toward the exterior wall. In this position it is parallel to the ceiling joists. The roll will probably unwind itself and end up at the other side of the room. Cut it off about 4″ longer than the distance across the room. Wedge the remaining roll between a couple of studs on the interior partition so that it does not unroll any further. Pick up the insulation from underneath the paper backing. Step up on your low scaffold plank or step ladder and proceed to tuck the blanket up between the joists. Staple the 1″ paper flange to the vertical surfaces of the sides of the joists. Make the outer edge of the flange flush with the lower edge of the joists. With two people working, one will lead out, stretch, and hold, while the second person staples. A T brace or two placed across the joists under the insulation will help immeasurably. It will require a staple about every 6 to 8″ to support the blanket, as friction fitting is not applicable in this position. Be certain that the beginning end is tightly compressed against the starter piece that was installed first above the plate. This is the most critical exfiltration place in the ceiling. Be very careful not to tear the paper with the nose of the stapler.

It is possible, though more involved, to put an uncut blanket across the full span of the ceiling. Such a practice is preferred where it can be accomplished. Lay the blanket roll on the other side of the interior bearing partitions, those parallel to the opposite exterior wall. Feed the starter end of the roll up into the attic while folding it lengthwise with paper out and down. With the aid of one or more helpers, carefully snake the blanket over any and all perpendicular partitions until the exterior-wall starting point is reached. Staple and work back toward the roll. Complete the job in the remaining area, making sure not to cut the piece short. The concluding end must compress and fit as well as the starting end. During the snaking, be careful not to tear the paper, as the main purpose is to sustain a continuous, leakproof seal throughout.

The first and last joist cavities, the ones on each end of the house, will be narrower than those in the field. Cut the blanket about 1" wider than the cavity width. The fiberglass will thereby compress snugly against the sides of the joists. Any small inconsistency in width will seldom result in a void.

Leave no secluded area without insulation. Be especially conscientious about small voids around chimneys, backer blocks, vents, and wiring. The smallest leak can allow exfiltration like air out of a punctured tire. It takes only a few voids to seriously damage the integrity of the whole system.

An attic access or a fold-down stair will account for significant loss unless insulated and weather sealed (Figs. 2-20 and 2-21). An

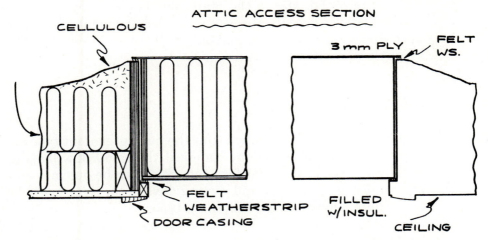

Figure 2-20 The attic access is insulated on a par with the ceiling by constructing a lightweight box filled with insulation and weather stripping around both upper and lower points of bearing.

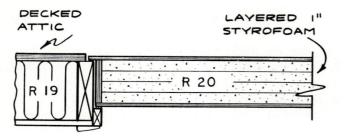

Figure 2-21 Using Styrofoam layers for the core of an access box will reduce the height of the box. The economical bead board type will net a value of about R-5 per inch of depth.

access with only a single piece of paneling or plywood on the opening is like a single-pane window. Build a box door as deep as the insulation depth surrounding it. Build a frame around the opening to hold the surrounding insulation away from the box. Fill the trapdoor box with insulation. Fasten a top board of light plywood on it. Let this top board hang over the box on all sides so that it rests on the opening sides. Place a weather-seal gasket between the box top and the top of the opening casement. Use a material such as felt. Foam rubber deteriorates rapidly in hot weather. Place another weather seal between the bottom of the box and the casement stop at the lower edge. The opening is now insulated and sealed against exfiltration.

Folding stairs are more difficult to insulate, though not impossible. A dense Styrofoam sandwich on the bottom face of the door will add some R value but will not be enough to equal the ceiling rating. A box above the stair comprised of several layers of dense Styrofoam will complete the requirement. It can be a push-up type or hinged to fold out of the way if there is adequate height under the rafters.

WALL INSULATION

Fiberglass batt insulation is by far the most prevalent type used in exterior wall cavities. By any standard, the payback will always be worth the installation cost for as much as can be put into an exterior wall where heating and cooling days of the year are substantial. There are two general blanket types available, vapor-barrier backed and friction fit. They also go by the terms "faced" and "unfaced."

The faced type has a reflective foil backing or an asphalt-impregnated vapor-seal paper backing. The foil is said to turn back heat rays. Both types will provide an effective moisture barrier when properly installed.

Good installation mandates completely filling the stud cavity. This will not be accomplished simply by stuffing the blanket into the opening, as the edges will catch here and there and compact, leaving unseen voids behind the edges. A putty knife or a paint stick sharpened like a chisel makes a good tool to push the edges of the fibers to the back of the cavity.

Carefully separate the blanket at the bottom where there is wiring to be enclosed (Fig. 2-22). Feed the back half of the insulation up, over, and down behind the wire and tuck it behind the duplex outlet box (Fig. 2-23). Cut a neat rectangle a little smaller than the box in the front half of the blanket and fit the insulation around the box. Do not shove the full-depth blanket in on top of a wire that crosses between studs or pull the full thickness down behind the wire. This is a sure way to reduce its effectiveness. Those

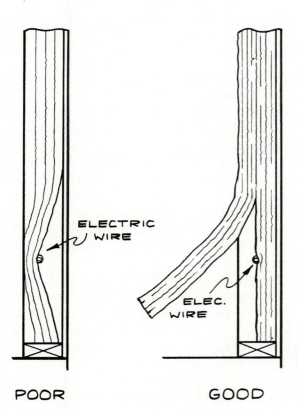

ELECTRIC WIRE

ELEC. WIRE

POOR   GOOD

Figure 2-22 Carefully separate the insulation blanket. Pull the back half down behind the electric wire.

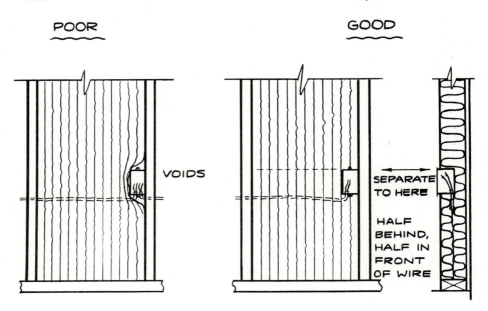

Figure 2-23 Great heat loss will occur around electric boxes that are not insulated correctly. Split the insulation and tuck half behind the box and wires that cross. Cut away a rectangle from the front layer where the box is.

cold-air drafts that come out of duplex outlets are certain signs of faulty insulating techniques.

Unlike the ceiling, which requires the paper flange to be stapled to the joists' vertical surfaces to provide sheer grip, the wall installation will not need this type of support. The paper flange is stapled to the facing edge of the stud. Line the 1″ flange edge up ½″ from the other side of the stud (Fig. 2-24). A total of five staples is adequate to keep the paper flat and taut. The leading edge can be held with less since it will be lapped ½″ by the succeeding blanket flange, and the staples from that flange will secure both pieces when placed in the center of the stud. This lineup provides a ½″ overlap of the flanges.

Precut stud-length batts are made a little longer than the opening so that the top of the blanket can be compressed up against the top plate. The paper will then lap onto the plate so that a couple of staples can be put in to support the blanket while stretching it taut and smooth.

Friction-fit batts come in stud lengths for nominal 4″-deep walls on 16″ centers. For 6″ stud walls on 24″ centering, the batts are most obtainable bagged in half-lengths. Start at the top and

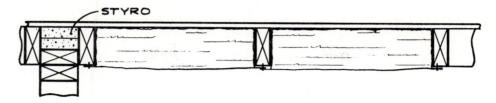

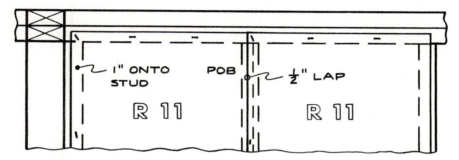

Figure 2-24   Lapping the vapor barrier paper correctly can save almost 50 percent of the staples. After the first stud (POB), staple through both paper edges simultaneously. Note the layered Styrofoam insulation in the intersection post behind the blocks.

press the batt in with some compression against the underside of the top plate. Fluff the side out and in so that the cavity is completely filled. Where using two-piece batts, be certain that the ends in the center touch snugly and contact is made with the plate at both top and bottom.

Insulate all other cavities that do not contain full batts or blankets. Custom fit the larger openings with cut pieces. Stuff all the small cracks that remain around window and door frames. Check corner posts and intersection posts. Leave no cavity without insulation, no matter how small or insignificant it may appear. Each void constitutes a future leak, a drain on the homeowner's purse.

PLASTIC VAPOR BARRIER

A vapor barrier for unfaced batts is made by draping sheet plastic over the entire wall. Start on the face of a partition stud with a full 100′ roll of 8′ plastic. Use as few staples as possible, but be certain that the plastic is held firmly to the top plate. It should cover the horizontal joint of the double plate to reduce the potential of infiltration. Make no cuts whatever in the entire roll. Run it over all windows, doors, electrical outlets, and any other openings. Do not cut these openings, except necessary entrances, until after the wallboard is installed. This system will produce a tight, well-held vapor barrier with little potential for leakage. After the drywall is on, it is a simple matter to cut around the inside of the window jambs with a knife. When the end of the roll is reached, lap a new roll over it. Cover a full stud cavity width (16″ or 24″) with the lap. Remember, do not cut or stop the plastic in each room. Run it over each partition intersection so that an airtight seal exists. The plastic will pucker a little going over the sole and a little more under the top plate. Slit the corner of the plastic on each side of the plate so that it can lie flat. Staple the corners down to the plates.

On a super-insulation design, where the objective is a totally leak free house, sheet plastic will also be used to cover the ceiling. It will take some ingenuity and conscientiousness to make it completely tight, as the plastic cannot be fed over partitions where trusses are used (the webs interfere). Each contact at the upper plates is made by permitting a fold of a couple of inches of plastic to run down onto the vertical face of the top plates. At the room corners, a fold is made like a paper package. Any damage to the plastic, such as a hole, should be sealed with nylon tape or plumber's tape. After the ceiling and wall skin are installed, each room will be a tightly sealed compartment, free of drafts and exfiltration.

There was a period in the history of building when it was thought that a house should breathe in order to dissuade condensation. Now it is known and accepted that a house need not be built to leak to achieve an absence of condensation. It can and should be built airtight for the sake of heating and cooling economy. The necessary periodical exchange of air that prevents condensation can then be controlled at will by the occupants rather than left to chance by leaky construction.

8 DRYWALLING

For many years prior to World War II, the most common wall coverings were wallpaper on top of plaster or textured and painted plaster. Wet plaster was spread over fuzzy, rough wooden lath.

These lath boards were about ⅜″ × 1¼″ × 40″. Lathing in the cities was a vocation all to itself. Watching a lather swing his hatchet hammer was like seeing a symphony in rhythm. He could set a nail and with a single whack drive it home through the lath into a stud. The hatchet hammer on the backstroke would revolve in his hand almost imperceptibly to the eye, coming forward with the hatchet side to sever the excess of the lath at a point dead center over the stud. It was done that way for centuries until gypsum lath was invented.

Wet plaster was applied in three separate coats. The first coat was called the *brown coat*. It was hairy and clung well to the lath. The second coat was the *scratch coat*. It was a finer-grade composition. While still wet and soft, it was striated in random swirls to create a uniformly roughened surface. The final topping coat was made of fine-grained lime. It was troweled to a smooth surface for wallpaper application or given some configuration for painting.

Wet plastering, as the system was called, was slowly phased out throughout the country. Except for specialty work, the craft has been replaced by the drywall system. The demise of wet plaster came primarily because of one poor construction feature that was eliminated by "drywall" (gypsum wallboard). The wet-plaster process took up about three weeks of the building schedule in lost time while waiting for the moisture to dry slowly. It was so humid in the house that new wood window casements would run water on the surface, soaking all the wooden parts. They would swell shut and delay the painting job interminably. All cabinet and trim work had to be delayed until the humidity reached a low enough level not to cause swelling. Some aesthetic features of the wet plaster era have been lost. Many homes of even modest budget had coved ceilings and arched passageways that are impractical to make with dry products. There is a nostalgia to some of these grand old homes, which should give the remodeler cause to pause and reflect before tearing them out and doing them over. The wet-plaster trade is not extinct. It can be located on demand, although it is now a specialty in the residential field.

PLASTER BOARD

Plaster board is a general term for gypsum board. Both are sheet forms of wall-covering board. The gypsum plaster is sandwiched between paper. As a building product for wall covering, it is universal. The most common type is faced with a manila vinyl-sealed paper. On the back side is a less costly gray paper. Other designs of gypsum wallboard are available with prefinished surfaces of wood-grain decals, fabric patterns, and wallpaperlike designs.

THE DRYWALL SYSTEM

The system of drywalling and the term **drywall** have become synonymous with gypsum board. In fact, few if any builders refer to the product as anything but drywall. As a system, drywalling means the installation of gypsum wallboard, followed by taping and leveling of joints with compound. The great advantage to the construction industry of drywalling over the wet-wall process is time. No time is lost. The drying time for the joint compound is usually overnight or, at most, a day or two in damp weather.

INSTALLING DRYWALL

For the most part, drywalling is an independent trade, although carpenters and handymen can and do install drywall sheets satisfactorily. The art of joint finishing, however, is a highly skilled operation and not often within the capability of the casual dabbler. It is a manipulative skill similar to the troweling of flatwork masonry.

    The sequence of drywall installation is from the top down. There is a definite logic in this order. The ceiling boards are placed and secured first. The wall boards are put on horizontally. The top course is placed and secured first so that its upper edge will support the edge of the ceiling board (Fig. 2-25). This also provides a cup joint on both edges (ceiling and wall) so that the joint tape and compound can have some depth and the corner will remain square. The lower wallboard is installed last. It is pressed tightly against the board above by the use of foot raisers or levers. The house constructed conventionally with precut studs will have a little extra height so that with two horizontal sheets and a ½″-thick ceiling sheet, all boards will go in without trimming the bottom sheet. A precut stud (92 ⅝″) plus a 2 × 4 sole (1½″) plus a double top plate (3″) adds up to 97⅛″. Theoretically, the ceiling board and two vertical wall boards take up 96½″ of height (less on the cupped side of

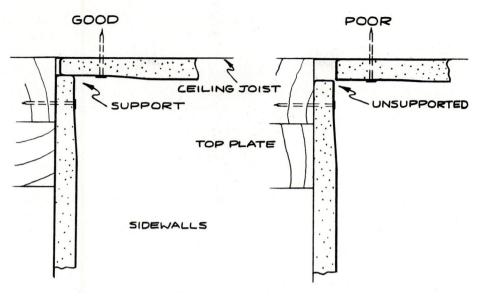

Figure 2-25   Ceiling sheets are installed first so that wall sheets will support them. Leave about ⅛″ clearance.

the ceiling board). In practice, all components—the floor and the top plate—would have to be perfectly straight and parallel to have ⅝″ of space left over. Such perfection is not the rule; therefore, the ⅝″ becomes a buffer zone to accommodate imperfections in alignment (levelness, plumbness, and parallelism).

DRYWALLER'S OBJECTIVES

Drywalling is one of the those seemingly simple jobs that can really be goofed up, or it can be accomplished reasonably well with knowledge and the desire to do a good job. Some stated objectives should set the stage for the latter. By careful adherence to the instructions and illustrations that follow in these pages, the learner will:

1. Know the preferred direction to place drywall sheets on the ceiling and walls.
2. Be able to make a bill of materials for a room or a full house.
3. Evaluate and establish the best cup joint and square-edged butt joint locations.

4. Know how to plot and arrange the most feasible-sized boards to cause the least number of end joints (there are no cups on the ends).

5. Know specific nailing and gluing patterns for different places.

6. Make cuts for length, width, electrical outlets, and openings to a tolerance of ⅛″ without tears or fractures.

7. Raise and secure boards with or without assistance using supporting aids.

8. Know the proper nails to use and how to seat and dimple them.

9. Know several methods of securing butt joints where no cupped edge exists.

WALLBOARD DIRECTION

Wallboards are placed perpendicular to joists and studs wherever the area is greater than 4′ × 8′. A surface that is no longer than a sheet may be covered with a single piece installed parallel to joists or studs, provided that it can be put in place. A 2′ × 4′ closet, for example, could have a single 4′ × 8′ sheet for the back wall and a 23½″ piece for each end cut lengthways from a full sheet. In this case there is no reason to cut a 4 × 8 in half, making two 4 × 4 pieces, just to form a horizontal joint at the center. Where a full sheet can be maneuvered into place, the necessity of taping and compounding a midheight joint is eliminated.

Ceiling placement of full and sublength boards follows some rules designed to minimize stress cracks. One of the most frequent callbacks on new construction is due to cracked end joints in ceiling drywall. There are two reasons for this, one of which has to do with proximity of joints (the other reason for joint failure is covered later under a discussion of how to make a strong end joint). Plan the whole ceiling arrangement before starting. Sketch a layout on paper to clarify the situation graphically.

Rooms under 16′ in length can and should be covered with full-length boards. This eliminates any end butt joints, a serious objective. Drywall is obtainable in 8, 10, 12, 14, and 16′ lengths. There is a trend away from 14 and 16′ lengths, as the weight and awkwardness of handling are objectionable. Nonetheless, if manpower is available, these lengths will provide the best job. Some yards stock only 8 and 12′ lengths. Assume for an example that 12′

is the longest available board and that the room to be covered is a rectangular shape 12′ × 18′ with ceiling joists spanning the 12′ direction. The first rule to keep in mind is to stagger the joints as far apart as possible *and* avoid any in the central area of the room. The center is the area of greatest flexibility of ceiling joists or truss chords. Any flexing from an imposed load will set in motion the possibility of a failed joint in this locality. See the diagrams shown in Fig. 2-26 denoting poor joint location and those indicating better joint location. A proper arrangement of sheets does not occur by chance, but must be planned. Determine where the first full sheet or nearly full sheet will be placed. Then mark all future end locations on the joists with a carpenter's red crayon or felt-tipped pen.

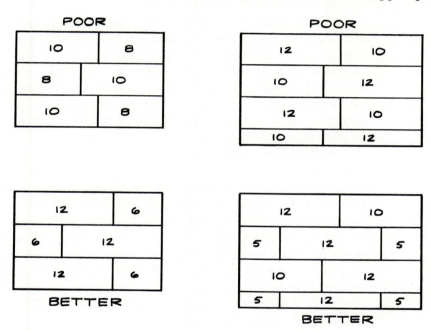

Figure 2-26 Joints should not be allowed to just happen. Place them to fall far apart and not in the central area of a large room. These rooms are 12 × 18 and 14 × 22.

PLOTTING THE MATERIALS

There are two ways of going about the business of mapping board location, estimating needs, and creating a bill of materials from which to order. One method is to do it piecemeal. One might compute the total square footage of all the wall and ceiling area in the house (the ceiling can be taken from the square footage on the floor plan). Do not discount doors and windows. Then order some common modules. For example, where 12′ is practical for the longest length, an initial order may be placed for as many sheets as would cover 75 or 80 percent of the total. Then begin the job. All ceilings are covered first. Cutoffs are carefully stacked. Each cutoff is used wherever possible. When the supply of boards is exhausted and none of the scraps left over will fit anywhere, an assessment of the remaining areas to be covered is made. This method is favored by those who shun the analytical planning exercise for its tedium or difficulty. A few dollars more for waste is considered well worth the cost to avoid the mathematics.

The analytical approach to estimating and making a bill of materials requires more planning. The main result is less waste of materials. Contractors often opt for the first method, except that an attempt will be made to order 100% of the estimated need, thereby producing a single invoice. The contract price is usually based on a square-foot cost of purchased material; therefore, waste becomes profit. By comparison, the lump-sum contract will be hurt by waste or overordering.

Individual room assessment is the first step in producing the detailed materials bill. A floor plan can be used on which to outline placements of sheets for each room. Bear in mind that each sheet will be placed at right angles to the ceiling joists. The cup joints usually run lengthways of a rectangular house. L-, T-, and U-shaped houses may have joists in the wings running at 90° to those in the main body of the structure. The actual direction must be known in order to plot the proper direction in which the ceiling sheets will be positioned.

The ceiling is actually plotted better from inside the house rather than from the plan. The best placement is more obvious when looking at the actual construction. Any question of lengths is readily answerable by counting joist spaces or by measuring the real distance.

Modular placement is the name of the game in the analytical method of computing drywall need. The project is a jigsaw puzzle where full modular pieces are inserted first, followed by segments. Start by working out the ceiling puzzle on paper for each room.

Next, lay the walls of the room out into a straight line as you would cut one corner of a box and fold it out flat. Draw it to scale or use ¼″ graph paper (let a ¼″ square equal 2′ × 2′). Draw the vertical lines where the corners of the walls are. Draw in the doorways. The bottom of the doorway may net a small saving in wallboard. Most windows may be ignored, as they usually cut into both the upper and lower sheets, for a total module loss. Only where a series of windows go down to the baseboard or floor can a saving be realized.

Place end joints above and below windows whenever possible, *never at the corners of openings* (Fig. 2-27). The header area above a window is usually an area of solid backing, which makes for a good drywall joint. Most windowsills are lower than the midpoint of the wall, so any end joint in the area below the sill will be shorter than if it were made elsewhere, where it would be a full 48″ high.

Code the foldout wall diagram with numbers indicating the

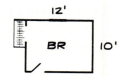

START AT A CORNER

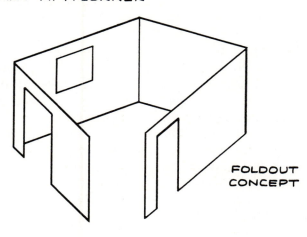

FOLDOUT
CONCEPT

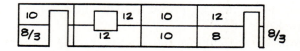

Figure 2-27 Make a foldout pattern layout for the walls of each room. Start the foldout at any corner. Label and code the laid-out pattern.

sheet length that is required to cover an area. Remember that this is a modular number game of units, not a square foot analysis. Several small segments that take less than a full sheet can be coordinated into a single sheet. A double number stated like a fraction is one way to code it. The top number is the sheet length from which the piece will be cut. The bottom number is the quantity of pieces coming out of that piece. All that remains is to label the schematic with a room description.

Accumulating a total ordering list is a simple matter of addition. Make a foldout schematic for each room. Add the sheets of each size required. Then total all room orders by sheet size. Do the same with the ceilings.

Why bother to order different lengths? Why not just order all long sheets? Several reasons are worth considering. One is the difficulty of handling the bigger sheets and the extra cutting that will be necessary. There will be a larger accumulation of subsized cutoffs to attempt to use. Added cost may also be a compelling consideration, as the larger sheets usually cost more per square foot.

CUTTING GYPSUM BOARD

There are a number of tools for cutting drywall, any of which will work adequately. There are some preferred tools for certain locations.

Cutting a straight piece off the end of a board or the edge is probably done best with a knife-edged tool (linoleum knife, drywall hatchet, pocket knife, etc.). Use a straightedge guide. A drywall square is effective up to 4′. Always cut away from the T of the square, as cutting toward it usually dulls your knife as it passes over the metal T. A leftover strip of plywood with one factory edge (the uncut original edge) makes a good 8′ straightedge. For the cleanest break, cut the board on both sides, especially when getting close to an edge or end (Fig. 2-28). The backside cut should be a little undercut so that the leading edge will be the face side. The little gypsum knobs that remain after breaking can be rasped off with a drywall rasp board or a coarse sandboard. Do not attempt to rasp away paper to shorten a board, as it will only fray and make a poor joint. If the paper needs shortening, use the straightedge and knife again.

It is not always necessary to cut the back side. On crisp, dry

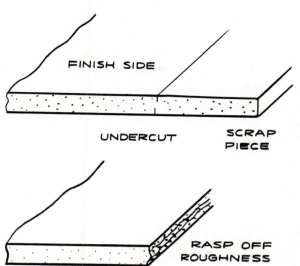

FINISH SIDE

UNDERCUT

SCRAP PIECE

RASP OFF ROUGHNESS

Figure 2-28 Cutting away a strip close to an edge is best accomplished by cutting both sides. Little knobs remaining may be rasped off.

days the board will be brittle. A cut line on the face side is usually adequate. The board is snapped gingerly in the same manner that glass is scarred and broken on a line. The scrap or smaller segment is folded back and a knife run down the valley.

To cut away the corner of an L-shaped piece, the cut must be made on both sides of the board (Fig. 2-29). The gypsum is

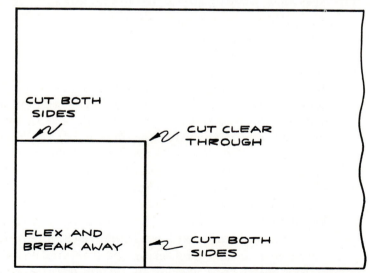

CUT BOTH SIDES

CUT CLEAR THROUGH

FLEX AND BREAK AWAY

CUT BOTH SIDES

Figure 2-29 To remove a corner, cut both finish and backside of the pattern, sever completely through at the corner, and flex the cutout until it falls free.

snapped and broken on one line first. Then it is snapped on the other line. A little flexing and the scrap corner piece can be eased away. A little insurance against tearing the paper beyond the corner intersection may be had by making sure that your knife penetrates completely through the gypsum at the intersection of the cut lines. Do not allow the cut lines to go beyond the corner, as this will encourage the break to do the same. Another technique to avoid inside corner-breaking problems is to press a drywall bayonet saw through at each leg of the corner and saw away from the corner about 1″. A woodworker's compass saw (often incorrectly called a keyhole saw) works well for this purpose.

MEASURING AND CUSTOM FITTING

When working with wood, it is advised that a board or panel to be fitted to an opening be cut a little long and then trimmed back to a precise fit. Such is not the case with drywall cutting. The difference is that the drywall system employs a fluid compound intended to fill voids, whereas gaping joints in wood patched with a filler are a sure sign of poor craftsmanship. There are other reasons for not fitting a long sheet of gypsum board tightly into an opening. Gypsum absorbs a lot of moisture, which causes swelling. A board on the ceiling or wall that touches at each end of the room cannot expand lengthwise, so its only alternative is to bow outward from one joist or stud to the adjacent one and sometimes cause "nail popping."

Labor saving will be realized by planned short-cutting wherever the end of a sheet butts a corner. Plan to allow a ⅛″ minimum clearance at the ends. For example, where a surface can be covered from one end to the other (an inside fitting), ⅛″ should be allowed at each end (Fig. 2-30). Therefore, the sheet will be cut ¼″ shorter than the actual measurement of the area length being covered.

Unsquare corners cause problems if the condition is ignored before cutting the wallboard. The squareness of corners can be monitored by measuring. A framing square can also be used, but its smallness can produce a faulty assessment. Check out the corner squareness by measuring the full length of a ceiling across the ceiling joists from corner to corner parallel and adjacent to the wall. Next move out from the wall 4′ and measure again, parallel

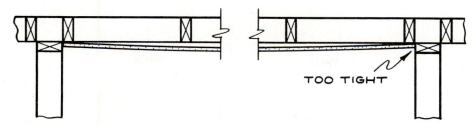

Figure 2-30 Cutting a board to the full dimension of an opening usually results in too tight a fit or crushed joints and broken corners. An ⅛″ clearance per mating edge is the rule. In the view shown, the board should have been cut ¼″ shorter than the distance between the partition frame.

to the first measurement. Where a room is perfectly rectangular or a parallelogram, the measurements will be identical. If it is trapezoidal, one measurement will be larger or smaller than the other.

Check each corner with the square when there is suspicion or evidence of out-of-squareness. The large door-hanging square, made from a plywood cutoff scrap, is an excellent tool for checking squareness. Where one corner of the ceiling is square and the other is not, start the installation against the square abutment end and custom angle cut the wallboard to the other end.

Bear an important element in mind about pattern cutting. If you are cutting the ceiling board on a table, it must be remembered that the lengths will be reversed from side to side when the face side of the board is up because on the ceiling the face side is down. Many a sheet has been miscut because the person doing the cutting forgot that the sheet will be revolved 180°, which reverses the sides.

CUTOUTS

Light-fixture cutouts can be located in a number of ways. Measuring is one of the poorest methods. It usually results in an oversized hole and a difficult patch job. One method is to put the panel up in place. Hold it with T bars. Press or pound with your hand around the electric box. Let the panel down. There should be some faint indentation marks that allow tracing a box or pattern. A similar method is to use a fine bead of dark caulking. Cut the nozzle of a new tube so that a very thin bead comes out. Apply a bead all around on the box edges. Press the panel into it. Colored chalk can also be used. Squeeze the plastic chalk bottle sharply so that a mist of chalk dust is blown onto the box edges. Enough of an outline will be transferred to the wallboard so that a real box can be traced onto the position. These impression methods have one good feature in common. They make it impossible to cut the box hole in completely the wrong location, as is often done when measurements are used.

Remove the box hole plug by first cutting the tracing with a knife. Since the pattern is on the back side, make the cut a little larger (about $\frac{1}{16}''$) than the pattern. Push the point of a knife until it just breaks through the face side at four places around the circle (or octagon). Turn the sheet up on edge or over. Retrace the outline by centering a box or a template between the four punched slots. Use the bayonet saw or keyhole saw to cut out the plug. Be very careful not to tear the paper. Some fixtures (porcelain, for example) just barely go beyond the box, so there is very little room for error. One-eighth inch is about maximum.

Wall-outlet cutouts may be removed in the same manner. One must be careful to secure the upper edge of the sheet tightly against the ceiling for boxes that are in the upper half of the wall. This can be done effectively by using two half-length T boards of 49″ height (Fig. 2-31). The top T bar is made 12 to 14″ long with a $\frac{5}{8}''$ groove about $\frac{1}{2}''$ deep. This length will permit it to slip between the common stud spaces ($14\frac{1}{2}$ or $22\frac{1}{2}''$ wide). The gypsum board is hoisted into place and held there until the little T boards are wedged under the edge in two balanced locations (approximate quarter-points).

Should the upper plate line at the ceiling dip down at any point, a decision will be necessary. A small dip near the center can be compensated for by positioning the board so that a crack of equal width appears at each end between the board edge and the ceiling. The center area should be touching tightly.

A crack in excess of $\frac{1}{8}''$ above each end of a top-course wallboard may be cause to cut the edge of the sheet to the actual contour of the ceiling. This contour can be drawn on the immobilized board by scribing a parallel line starting at the edge of the board opposite the widest gap (Fig. 2-32). Hold something under the pencil to space it out to this point (your finger, a pencil compass, a chip of wood). With the other end of the pencil against the ceiling, draw it clear across the length of the board, making a mark parallel to

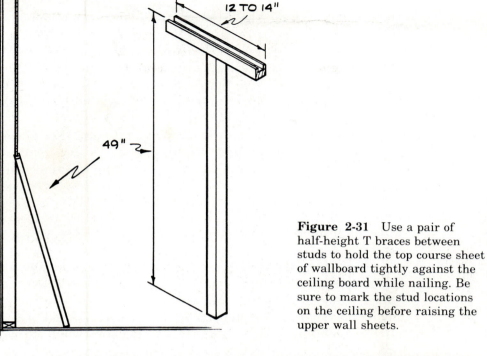

12 TO 14"

49"

Figure 2-31 Use a pair of half-height T braces between studs to hold the top course sheet of wallboard tightly against the ceiling board while nailing. Be sure to mark the stud locations on the ceiling before raising the upper wall sheets.

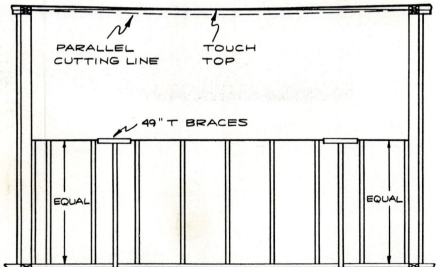

PARALLEL CUTTING LINE

TOUCH TOP

49" T BRACES

EQUAL

EQUAL

Figure 2-32 Mark a cutting line parallel to a plate line that is bowed down or up or crooked. Custom cut the edge to fit the irregularity. The lower edge should be parallel to the floor when making the contoured mark. The illustration is exaggerated for graphic clarity.

the ceiling. Kick out the T boards at the bottom while holding onto
the sheet. Lower it carefully. Cut precisely on the line. It will be
necessary to cut both sides, bearing down with considerable pressure to reach the center of the gypsum. It is not possible to break
off a slim piece like this with a cut on the face side only because
there is a double layer of paper on the back side where the gray
paper laps over the manila paper.

   Small gaps between the top wallboard and the ceiling board
can be filled with compound and allowed to dry before taping.
Larger ones will take multiple fillings, as each application will
shrink. This delays the job for 24 hours. It is simpler to custom fit
the edge than to do an extensive filling job. Any gap over $\frac{1}{16}''$
should be filled a day before taping begins. Failure to do so will set
up a condition for breakdown by leaving a void (an air pocket) behind the tape.

   Marking boxes in the lower half of the wall is done in a similar manner. Instead of T boards, a metal foot lever called a drywall
raiser is used (Fig. 2-33). Makeshift raisers can be made by planing a long bevel on the end of a 1 × 6 or a 1 × 8 board. A 1 × 1 or a
strip of molding can be nailed across the board about 2" back from
the bevel to form a fulcrum. The wallboard is brought into position
with the upper edge under the edge of the top wallboard, which has

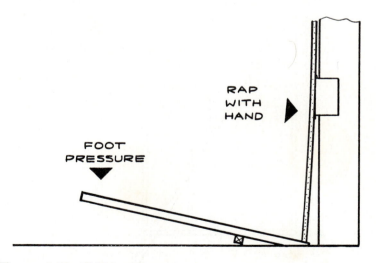

Figure 2-33   Hold lower panel up snug against the edge of the top
panel with foot lifter. Rap the board sharply over the box to form an
impression on the back side.

already been installed above. The raiser(s) are jammed against the sole plate with the wallboard on top of them. The installer then steps on the raiser with heel pressure and snugs the board up tightly to the board above. The board is not immobilized as the one above was. It must be held there until someone can establish the electrical outlet box impressions on the backside.

After all cutouts have been removed, the board is again put in place and nailed. The upper board, with its pair of supporting T board braces, will stay in place while nailing proceeds. The lower board must be held up or blocked up until a sufficient quantity of nails is installed to support the weight. This quantity is dependent on the size of the board. Place the first nails anywhere along the bottom or at marked locations in the field. Do not place the first nails along the top edge, as the board will tear away from them under the weight should the support be relaxed too soon.

The height of switch and duplex boxes is somewhat standardized but not mandatorily so. Some electricians stand the duplex box on top of their hammer. Some measure. Duplexes are usually between 12 and 16" above the floor level. The rule is *consistency*. Place them all at a uniform height.

Switch boxes are most conveniently set with the top at 48$\frac{9}{16}$" below the ceiling joists. A ½" gypsum ceiling will then position the box a small fraction of an inch below the bottom edge of the top wallboard. This makes it possible to saw or cut out just three sides of the box opening from the top edge of the bottom board. It also simplifies marking the location, as the box is clearly visible and traceable at the top of each side of the box. Hold a spare box up to these marks and trace around the three sides. For any other thickness of ceiling, the box will be set 48" plus the ceiling thickness down from the top of the plate.

Duplex outlet boxes for countertop appliances in the kitchen and bathroom are usually installed at a height of 40" (Fig. 2-34). Standard countertop height is 36". The backsplash may extend as much as 3 to 4" above the counter. The duplex faceplates should clear the backsplash. They can also be placed at the same height as switch boxes for the sake of standardization.

Specialty outlets may be designated on a plan at any specific height to meet a need. Regular duplexes along the walls of living rooms and bedrooms will not be labeled with height figures. Any other outlet that is not installed at this lower uniform height will have a definitive height dimension next to the duplex symbol.

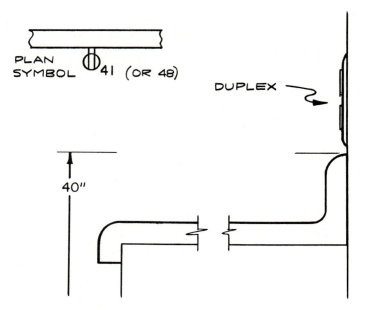

Figure 2-34 Duplex outlets other than those 12 to 16″ above the floor are marked with an inch designation indicating the distance from the floor to the bottom of the box.

Without this height callout (given in inches), the electrician will assume that the box is to be installed at the low standard level of 12″.

Strengthening the midpoint horizontal joint of the wallboard can be achieved in a number of ways. There was a time when 2 × 4 blocks were nailed between the studs to back up the joint area; however, the block is an objectionable obstruction to a good insulation job. It is an unnecessary cost item and is time-consuming to install. It came about partly as a vestige of the old firestop block used in balloon framing and later as a centering spacer. Some things are not questioned and just keep on happening long after the the need has disappeared.

A simple and economical way to stiffen the horizontal edge joint, which will later be taped and compounded, is to run a bead of panel adhesive along the top of the lower sheet just before it is pressed up against the other sheet. Go down the junction as soon as the nailing is supportive and flex the boards in or out at any location between studs where the edges do not line up perfectly. The edges can be flexed into perfect alignment. In a few seconds, the adhesive will immobilize the joint. Use a thin bead of adhesive, as squeeze-out is undesirable. Squeezed-out adhesive will interfere with the taping operation. Some installers prefer carpenter's glue to panel adhesive, as it can be mopped smooth with a wet finger, thereby eliminating hard beads that protrude later.

Kitchen and bathroom wallboard positioning presents a unique potential. The center-line joint can often be eliminated completely where there are long lengths of wall covered by upper and lower cabinets. The exposed area between the upper and lower cabinetry encompasses the normal location of the horizontal wallboard joint. A half-sheet of board, cut lengthways, is installed on the upper quarter of the wall, followed by a full-width sheet through the middle half-sector of the wall. The bottom quarter of the wall is covered with the remaining half-cut sheet. All the joints are now underneath (behind) the cabinets (Fig. 2-35). These joints should be taped and compounded to bring the surface to a straight line and to assure an infiltration-proof joint on the exterior walls. Backing or immobilizing with adhesive is unnecessary, as no pressure will ever be exerted against the joint. The resulting joint-free area between the cabinets presents a smooth, uniform surface, free of compound, for papering, tiling, or whatever covering is desired. The same technique can be used in a bathroom or laundry room where long cabinets are planned.

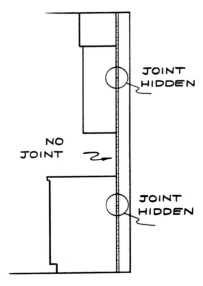

Figure 2-35 Behind cabinets that run the full length of a wall, a joist at midpoint can be eliminated by splitting a wallboard and placing half at the top, a full sheet through the middle, and a half at the bottom.

Tub and shower enclosures should be fitted with water-resistant wallboard with the closed cupped edge adjacent to the top flanges of a tub or shower. This vulnerable area should never have a raw, exposed gypsum edge on the wallboard. Even the papered edge should not be resting tightly against a tub surface. A ⅛″ gap is provided so that a channel will exist to fill with a waterproofing seal. Due to this exactness, this sheet is put on first (Fig. 2-36). The remaining area above must be carefully custom fitted. Measurements are taken at each end. The board is cut close enough to slip in snugly at top and bottom. The cut edge will be at the top. Remember the reverse orientation problem when laying out the cut. Even though a straightedge is to be used, it will be prudent to pencil mark the cut line the full length of the board. This will help eliminate a false cut should the straightedge slip during the cutting process.

Do not custom cut wallboards to fit around openings in a wall. Most cutouts for these locations will leave a board in an L or U shape. Such a piece is vulnerable to breakage from the inside corners out when it is being moved into position. A better method in most cases is to nail an uncut piece over the opening and then cut out the opening (Fig. 2-37). A drywall saw is held against the rough frame and worked toward the corner of the frame until the scrap falls away into your free hand. A doorway presents ready ac-

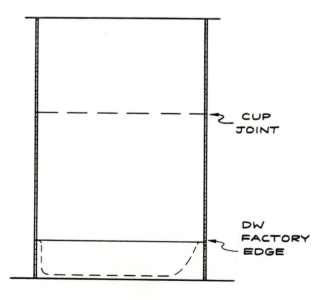

CUP
JOINT

DW
FACTORY
EDGE

Figure 2-36 Lay the first sheet of water-resistant wallboard with its closed factory edge along the tub rim. Custom cut and fit the pieces above.

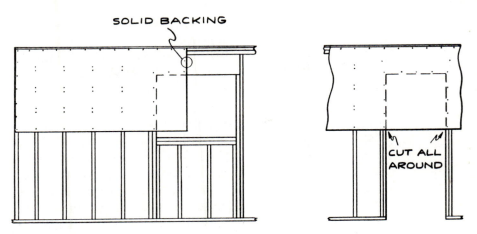

Figure 2-37   Saw out a window opening. Cut both sides of an interior door opening, flex, and pop it out.

cess to both sides of the overhanging board. A neat way to cut this piece out is with a knife and a straightedge on the face side. The upper corner can be accurately located on the face by punching a nail through the back side at the intersection of the header and trimmer. The back side is cut quickly simply by drawing the knife along the edge of the trimmer stud and the header. After both sides are cut, the board is wobbled to and fro until it falls away. An advantage of this method is a reduction in plaster dust (a characteristic of sawing).

FRAMEWORK SURFACE PREPARATION

Now that the reader has some background on installation sequence and placement of sheets, it becomes important to learn the techniques that make the difference between a neat job and a shoddy project. The wet-plaster system has one advantage over the drywall system. Wet plaster can be molded to cover up most of the minor obstructions and depressions that are found on framework. For the finished surface of drywall to appear flat and straight, it is required that the framework below be flat and straight. Corners, junctions, and parallel pieces of wood must meet as intended without obtrusions, depressions, or misalignment. This factor places a much higher requirement on the accuracy and quality of the so-called rough framework.

Each surface to be covered must be carefully inspected for any type of imperfection that will affect the ultimate surface and alignment of the drywall (Fig. 2-38). A stringline should be used to check the ceiling flatness across the joists and diagonally. There may be a joist with its crown reversed (down), which must be flexed up and held with a strong back. Occasionally, a truss web is misaligned, which malforms the lower chord relation. It has to be detached, reset, and regusseted. Knots close to the edge of joists and studs are common causes of trouble. The protrusion is discovered by holding a long straightedge, such as a 4 or 6' level, against each board. The hump must be sawed to a straight line. Protruding nail heads should be driven flush to the surface. *Cupped headers* over windows and doors frequently protrude at the corners or center. Each protrusion must be eliminated (Fig. 2-39 a and b).

Earlier in the text the importance of not splitting the ends of plates was stressed. A split plate must expand to the interior and/or exterior. The widened board will hang over. Such an overhang on the interior must be cut off (a difficult job in the inside corner).

A thorough inspection, room by room, and marking with a red crayon is the layout forerunner to success. Mark a whole room as a unit. Then proceed methodically to make all the necessary corrections.

Phasing the surface preparation can be multistage. Where there is a large quantity to be done on the interior surfaces of the

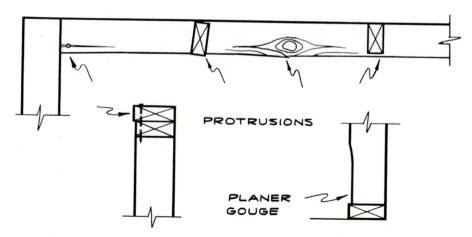

Figure 2-38 All protrusions and subsurface areas of significance should be leveled by removing or filling.

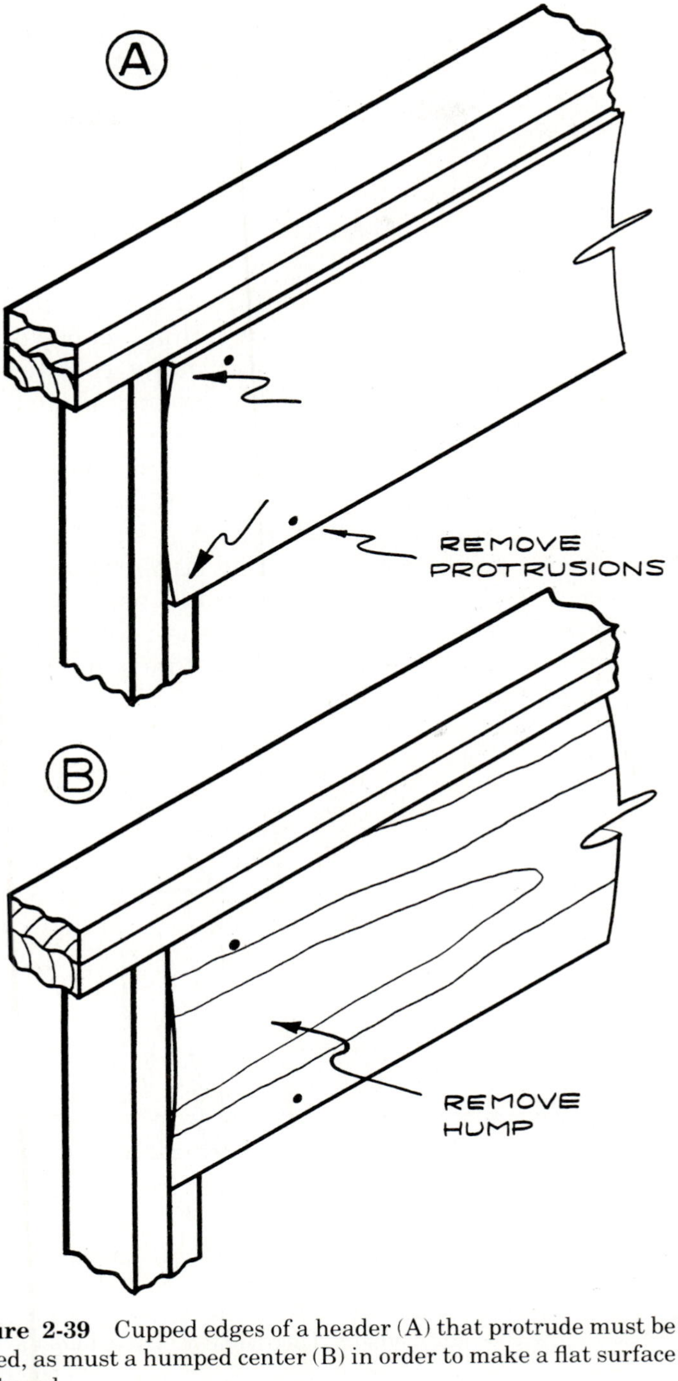

Figure 2-39 Cupped edges of a header (A) that protrude must be removed, as must a humped center (B) in order to make a flat surface for wallboard.

exterior walls, it will be accomplished more easily before the insulation is installed. The same is true for the ceiling. By contrast, the interior partitions may be left until just before the application of the drywall.

CEILING END JOINTS

There are three successful methods of butt joining the uncupped ends of gypsum board on a ceiling. There is one notoriously poor method, which accounts for many contract callbacks (defective work that fails within the warranty period).

The poor butt joint is one that meets end to end on the underedge of a single ceiling joist or lower truss chord (Fig. 2-40). This board presents a nailing surface of 1½". *If all conditions were perfect*, squareness of the room, straight coursing of the drywall sheets, perpendicularity, and straightness of the joists, the end of each gypsum board sheet would bear on a scant ¾" surface for nailing. Since perfect conditions rarely, if ever, exist, one or the other of the sheet ends will be short-changed as to nailing base. It is common to find failed joints with ½" or less backing. The plaster

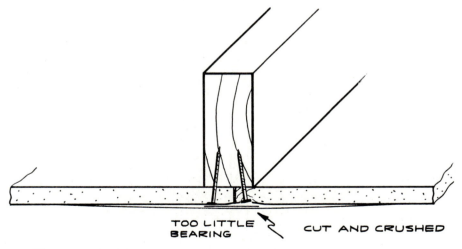

TOO LITTLE BEARING   CUT AND CRUSHED

Figure 2-40 This poorly conceived end joint is the cause of many warranty callbacks. Crushed gypsum, nail-cut paper, and uncentered nailing surface make it the poorest choice available. The protrusion of the tape and compound are usually visible under artificial light. Hairline cracks and complete separations are common to this joint design.

is usually fractured around the nails from attempted dimpling (setting of the head below the surface too close to the edge).

Another fault of this method is the basic nonfeasibility of the square edge butt, which does not provide a cup (recession) for the finish joint taping. Such a taped joint must be taped and compounded above or beyond the common surface (actually below the ceiling line). Attempts are made to taper this downward humping joint cover so that it will not show. The compound is said to be "feathered out." The result is a wide compounded area with a depth of material held to a minimum. There are two problems. Any flexing or slight vibration of the ceiling causes the tape to rupture or peel and a hairline crack appears. The alternating dryness and moisture in the air then begin the process of loosening the tape. From there on it is all downhill until reparation time. This constitutes one of the most difficult reparation jobs in a warranty. It can be done with complete satisfaction only by using two new joints on both sides of the joist, made as in method 1 (described later).

The second fault with the square butt surface joint is that it is readily discernible at certain times of the day and night. It sticks out like a localized sag when lights create a shadow area on the far side of the bulge. Under artificial light, one can easily locate the joints and identify the sheets on the ceiling. Attempts are often made to mask this undesirable condition by spraying a heavy coat of spatter finish on the ceiling. Spatter coating is attractive but will not solve the problem of a basically flawed joint. For those who will not be dissuaded from using the poorest joint, the only saving grace is to use an adequate adhesive under the butt joint.

Objectives of butt joining the ends of gypsum board sheets should include three items. First, locate the joint in a place or manner that creates the least vulnerability to stress that may result in failure. Second, support the joint permanently. Third, form a recess for tape and compound that is comparable to the cup-edge system on the long sides of the sheets.

Contrary to popular belief, a joint positioned or suspended between two structural framework members will meet the objectives more successfully than a joint placed over solid wood. Such a joint is illustrated in the United States Gypsum manual. Method 1, described next and shown in Fig. 2-41, places the joint in the middle quadrant between the ceiling joists. In this position the flexing of the joists under load or vibration is absorbed by the joists but not transferred to the drywall joint. Many drywall installers reject this

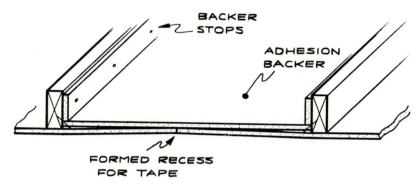

Figure 2-41   This is the best method of joining board ends between joists.

technique, due to the time and nuisance factor. The sad truth is that a poor job often results in a warranty callback and the nasty job of doing over what could have been done right initially.

Method 1. Plan to make the sheet ends butt somewhere near the center of the space between the ceiling joists (Fig. 2-41). The board ends that extend beyond the joists must have a little flexibility in order to form a recess for tape and compound (a substitute for the missing cup). The closer the joint is to the center of the space, the more flexible the end of each board will be. Obviously, this system will work better with joists or chords on 24″ spacing than with those on 16″ spacing since about four more inches of wallboard can be hung over.

Assemble the parts in the following order. Assume ½″ drywall for a ceiling.

1. Nail cleats to the sides of the joists ⅝″ above the lower surface of the joists.

2. Toenail a horizontal drywall backer board against the lower edge of the cleats.

3. Spread a continuous bead of adhesive in a serpentine pattern (or parallel lines) about 1″ apart, perpendicularly back and forth across the joint area.

4. Install both sheets of drywall rapidly. Space the nails closer together on the joists adjacent to the butt joint.

5. Position a T brace to press evenly and equally against each side of the joint. Press (prestress) the joint a little more than ⅛″ above the ceiling line. Leave the T brace in place overnight

if possible or at least until the adhesive has become rigid enough to support the bent-up ends of the two wallboards.

All the backup materials may be scrap if scrap is available. The cleats serve only to keep the backup board from being pushed up. Any small piece of wood strip will suffice. Even ½″ × ¾″ strips will do where enough canted nails are used. Drywall strips about 3″ wide will suffice if one edge is straight and square (the cup-edged scrap is preferred).

On a single house job, where there is no scrap pile at the out-set, the first few back boards will be cut from a full sheet. Frequently, a sheet is dropped on a corner and damaged at unloading time. That is the sheet to use. Cut off from the end a backer that is 14½ or 22½″ wide to fit the joist spacing that exists.

Drywall adhesive drys on its surface very quickly. Enough T braces should be readied so that both sheets of ceiling board can be raised and secured without delay. Five T braces are usually adequate, two for each sheet and one under the joint. Concentrate most attention on getting the joint prestressed and pressed as quickly as possible; then go back and complete the field nailing. Of course, the boards must be accurately positioned and secured with a few nails to be certain that no overlaps or gaps are created before securing the end joint.

At first glance at Fig. 2-41, it may appear that bending up the stiff ends of the drywall would create a leverage that would tend to pull down the backer board. This is true up until the adhesive solidifies. Once it has hardened, it partially fills the gap next to the joist so that the pressure no longer exists. Also, gypsum has no memory or grain stresses. After it has been in the curved profile for a few hours, it will stay that way permanently with no stress.

If the T brace supporting the joint is needed elsewhere, it may be possible to remove it after a few hours. One can test the adhesion of the joint by gently starting to remove the brace. Flex the middle of the brace pole while pushing out the bottom with your foot (Fig. 2-42). Keep an eye on the joint area. If the joint ends do not appear to move downward more than the amount they were prestressed, the brace may be removed.

After the brace is removed, an inverted valley will exist. Taping and compounding may proceed as for a cupped joint. It will take more compound, however, as the depression extends farther than the width of two mated cups. If one desires to see or know in

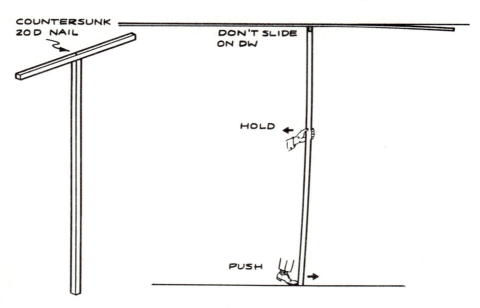

Figure 2-42 Place the T where desired. Hold in place with your hand. Push the bottom away with your foot until the T bar is wedged tightly under the sheet.

advance how far the feathering should go, a straightedge is laid across the depression and drawn across the ceiling boards. The outer edges of the depression may be marked for future reference to show the minimum boundaries for filling and feathering.

After the first and second steps of taping and compounding, a final coat of compound is screeded across the joint. The longest possible trowel is desirable for this final leveling, as the objective is to produce a flat surface from one joist to the other on the ceiling line. High spots can be sanded off using a long sandboard (16″ or more). Once perfected, this joint will be sturdy and virtually undetectable.

Method 2. The next best joint is made by creating a recess and adding a backer board on a joist. Each joint in a room should be established, marked, and prepared before starting to hang the ceiling board. Mark each 4′-wide junction with a red carpenter's crayon. Mark a line across the joist at each end of the joint location, then add a squiggly line along the joist from crossmark to crossmark.

Cut a 3/32 to 1/8″ deep recess from the underside of the joist or chord on all marked localities. This can be accomplished in one pass effectively with a hand power plane. Making this cut with a skillsaw is also effective but should be attempted only by the most experienced operator as working overhead is a dangerous operation with a skillsaw. Every precaution is advised, including safety goggles (not glasses) and a solid floor scaffold of ample width and length.

If the cut is rough and not too straight, the high spots can be smoothed off with a hand plane. Do not permit the recess to become deeper than ⅛″. Remember that the depth of the recess is what determines the quantity of compound to make the tape joint.

Next rip a 2 × 2 to a length a few inches over 4′ (Fig. 2-43). *Glue and nail* it flush with the recessed surface on the face of the joist. Use at least six 10d common nails spaced equally apart. Stay 2 or 3″ away from the ends of the 2 × 2 to avoid splitting. Lay the wider side of the 2 × 2 against the joist. The glue is most important.

The objective of the backer is to provide a more adequate nailing base for the end of each sheet of gypsum board. With the added 1½″ of wood, the bearing surface is now 3″. Glue each ceiling board to the joists with two or three beads of adhesive and space

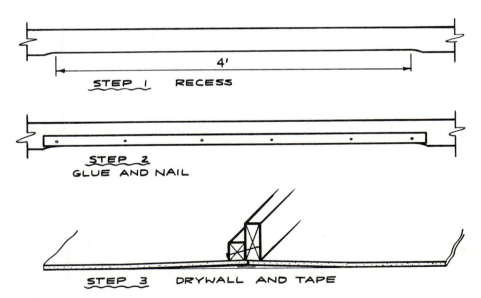

Figure 2-43 Planing and scabbing the joist provides a recess for the taping and compounding of an end butt joint. The depth of the cut (³⁄₃₂ to ⅛″) is exaggerated in this illustration for graphic clarity.

the nails no farther than 4" apart. Drywall screws may be 6" to 8" apart on this joint.

In a long room, or any room, where two or more joints will be made in the same course, the cleats are placed on the same relative sides of joists. This placement will maintain the modular spacing continuity so that full-length sheets can be installed without cutting or without running short. With the addition of the cleats, all ceiling board ends will have up to 1½" of nailing surface.

Use a T brace a couple of inches back from each joint before attempting to nail the drywall ends. Pressure must be exerted all along the end of each board while the nailing proceeds. Without this constant overall pressure, the ceiling board may break away downward from each nail as it is singly installed. After all nails are seated, a single T brace may be positioned to straddle the joint, thereby sustaining the pressure on the adhesive (Fig. 2-44). This will free one T brace for use elsewhere. The waiting period before

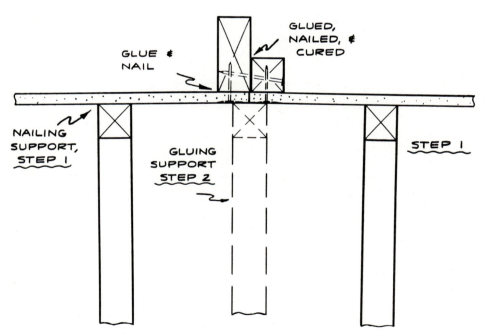

Figure 2-44 Use a brace on each side for solid contact while gluing and nailing the boards. Place a semipermanent T support over the joint *before* removing the outer two. Leave in place until the type of adhesive used is firmly set.

removing all pressure will be shorter than in method 1, where no fasteners were used.

Method 3. The last adequate method involves a recess with only minimum bearing (Fig. 2-45). Where joist or chord spacing is nearly perfect and perpendicular to the walls and partitions, it will be possible to come close to a full ¾″ contact of the end of each drywall sheet with the joist.

The procedure is carried out in three simple steps.

1. Locate and mark all joint locations.
2. Cut the recess gain at each location.
3. Glue, butt, and nail both ceiling board ends on the 1½″ bearing to complete the joint.

Omit the dimpling of nailheads. The nails will be so close to the end of each ceiling board that it is nearly impossible to dimple the nailhead without fracturing the gypsum. The recess made in the joist will usually be deep enough to allow space for compounding and taping over the surface-aligned nailheads. T braces are required as in method 2.

Adhesive is of paramount importance in all three joining methods because the boards are sprung up. In method 1, a large quantity of adhesive is involved. In method 2, there is adequate

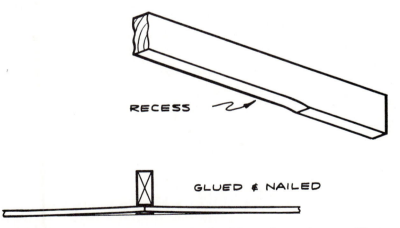

RECESS

GLUED & NAILED

Figure 2-45 This technique ranks third from the good to poor illustrations shown thus far. With perfect centering of the joint, good gluing technique, and nailing that does not cut the paper or crush the gypsum, the possibility exists for long, trouble-free existence.

surface to run two or three beads for each ceiling board. Method 3 offers the least surface area (¾″ or less for each board end); therefore, attention must be given to meticulous and effective coverage with adhesive. The success of this minimum method will depend largely on the effective holding power of the adhesive.

Supporting the cupped joint edges between ceiling joists may be accomplished by installing blocks *before* drywalling begins, or if joints are tight enough, by using panel adhesive on the edges (Fig. 2-46). All fitting must be done before spreading the adhesive head.

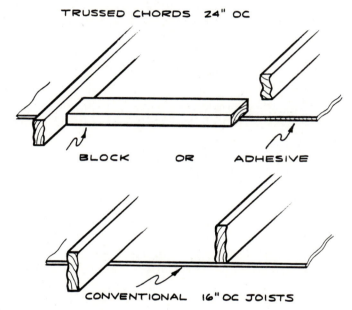

Figure 2-46 The joints running across the ceiling joists may be nailed to backer blocks or bonded together with adhesive. The bonding technique is usually adequate for the narrower 16″ conventional spacing. The wider 24″ spacing typical of trussing will benefit substantially from blocking to which the cup is edge nailed or from a continuous bead of panel adhesive. It may be necessary to support edges that do not align perfectly by placing a T brace in the middle of the span for a few minutes.

BUTT-JOINED WALL JOINTS

Where drywall is positioned horizontally on walls and partitions, there will be several end joints to deal with. An objective is to minimize full 4′ end junctions by preplanning the arrangement of full sheets so that joints come above doors and windows and below windows. By so doing, an upper-course joint, in particular, can be held to about 14″ in vertical height (the approximate distance from the ceiling line to the top of the window). Any window that is tall enough to have its sill below the top sheet of drywall will also produce a butt joint area of less than full 4′.

In larger rooms or where long expanses of unbroken partition exist, a full 4′-high joint may be unavoidable. There are three alternatives open to the drywaller.

Alternative 1. Install 8′-long drywall sheets vertically. There will be no butt joints without cupped edges on the surface. There is nothing objectionable about this method, but be prepared to defend your logic and rationale, as there are few old-timers around who will understand it. Also, remember to *stagger the vertical joint location of sheets* on the opposite side of the partition. Joints should not be present on both sides of the same stud, as this permits a flexibility weakness in the system.

Alternative 2. Install long sheets horizontally (Fig. 2-47). End the sheet at the center of a stud. Butt the next sheet tightly to the first. Surface bond the Perf-A-Tape. Cover it and feather it out broadly in the hope that it will not be noticeable and that the thin layer of compound will not crack. Stagger the sheets in the adjacent course. A joint weakness is created if one joint is above another on the same stud.

Alternative 3. Follow the design of method 1 used on the ceiling. End the sheets midway between the two studs. Fabricate with cleats and backerboard and adhesive. Place a ⅛″ × ¾″ strip straddled over the joint (Fig. 2-48). Staple it in three or four places so that it stays put. Place a ¾″ piece of plywood that is 20 to 24″ wide and 4′ high over the strip. Two to four inches of this board will lap beyond the studs on either side of the joint. Nail the plywood board over the wallboard to the studs with eight form nails (double-headed) of 12d size. Use four nails per side. Set all eight nails so that the points are protruding slightly through the underside before placing the board on the wall. Each nail will be positioned in a row of four on the long side of the plywood, parallel and 16″ apart from the other row. Their formation is such that each nail will anchor in a stud. Start the nails closest to one end about 5″ away from the end. This will help prevent them from splitting the ends of the studs adjacent to the plates. The other nails are placed equidistantly apart.

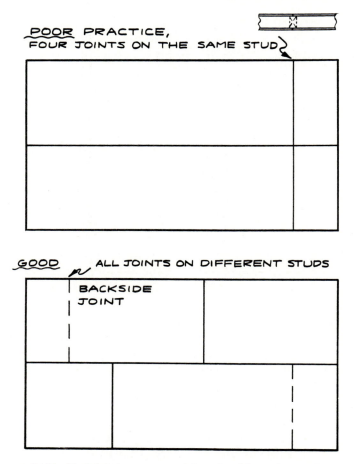

POOR PRACTICE,
FOUR JOINTS ON THE SAME STUD

GOOD   ALL JOINTS ON DIFFERENT STUDS

BACKSIDE
JOINT

Figure 2-47 End joints on a partition should not be made on the same stud on the same surface or on the opposite side of the wall. Of the possible four joints, no more than one per stud is the rule, as shown here.

Install the board over the stapled strip. Nail all of one vertical side first. Drive the nails only until the board touches the wall-board. Do not overpound. Apply pressure to the other vertical edge with your subdominant hand and sink the remaining nails. It may take a second person to do the pressuring on dry days when the board is very stiff. When the plywood is flush with the surface, the little spacer strip underneath will have depressed the wallboard enough to provide a recess for tape and compound, netting a completely masked joint. For permanence and best looks, alternative 3 is the best joint to use. Future convenience is also attained because

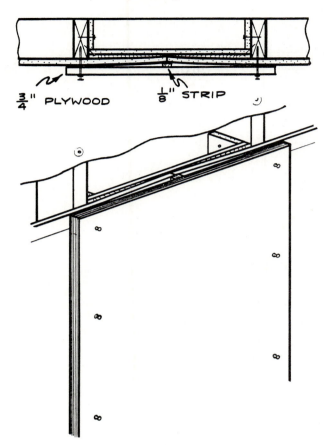

$\frac{3}{4}$" PLYWOOD $\frac{1}{8}$" STRIP

Figure 2-48 This recommended wall joint between studs is completely concealable after the temporary pressure board is removed. The pressure-board technique works equally well on the ceiling in place of the T brace.

baseboard trim will not have to be relieved (planed on the back side) in order to pass straight over a built-up hump of compound. Nor will the compound have to be cut away from behind the baseboard (the alternative to baseboard relieving). Leave the board in place overnight. Remove carefully with a wrecking bar by pulling the form nails. A set of boards, removed with care, may be used repeatedly. The eight nailholes remaining in the drywall are simply filled with compound.

SUCCESSFUL NAILING OF GYPSUM BOARD

Nailing would seem to be elementary, but the sad fact is that some drywall installations are unsuccessful due to poor nails or poor installing technique (Fig. 2-49). Several elements affect the holding

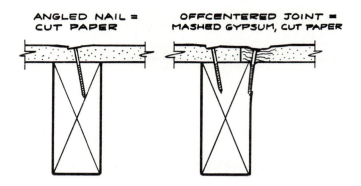

ANGLED NAIL =   OFFCENTERED JOINT =
CUT PAPER   MASHED GYPSUM, CUT PAPER

POOR NAILING

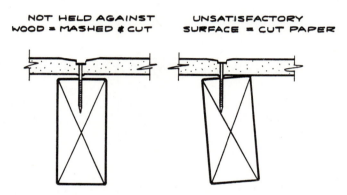

NOT HELD AGAINST   UNSATISFACTORY
WOOD = MASHED & CUT   SURFACE = CUT PAPER

Figure 2-49   Poor nailing technique is often the cause of a future drywall failure, particularly with ceilings that depend solely on nails.

power of nails used with drywall. They are the species of wood into which the nails anchor, the type of nail, the positioning and frequency of nails, and the expertise with which the nail is installed.

Wood species use has changed in the past half-century. Until World War II, there was little concern for conservation of timber. Structural members of a house were generally high grade and of harder wood than found today. Lath nails were smooth and gunmetal blued. In the heavy, dense wood studs and joists, the nails held well. After the war, the lumber supply and the timber forests began to be depleted rapidly. Softer woods of less adequate strength and nail-holding ability were put on the market. The drywall system was becoming popular at about this same time. The problem of popouts soon reared its ugly head. The steel industry responded with an annular ringed nail that has superior holding power in soft wood. Carpenters quickly dubbed it a "ring shank," Annular nails are currently available in sizes from the mighty barn pole nail down to the diminutive panel nail.

A true drywall nail in its purest form is ringed along all the portion that will be anchored in the wood (Fig. 2-50). Maximum holding potential is thus guaranteed. There are other forms on the market labeled drywall nails. One is a nail with a head large enough to qualify but no rings. For holding power, this nail is hot dipped in galvanizing tanks. The resulting rough encrustation on the shank of the nail gives it some superiority over a smooth nail.

Some recent imports masquerading under the box label of drywall nails are nothing more than 4d nails with slightly larger heads and resin coating. The resin is of doubtful benefit because it is partly stripped away and its adhesiveness nullified as it passes through the gypsum.

A good test of the efficiency of these three types of nails is to nail a scrap of drywall to a 2 × 4 with two or three nails of each design. Pull them out successively. It will be quite obvious which is superior.

Positioning the nails has also undergone transition (Fig. 2-51). In the beginning, the drywall sheets were installed vertically. All nails were installed an equal distance apart, those on the cup edge and those in the field. After gypsum-board hanging evolved to the horizontal position on the walls, it was found that holding power was improved by grouping the nails in pairs 2″

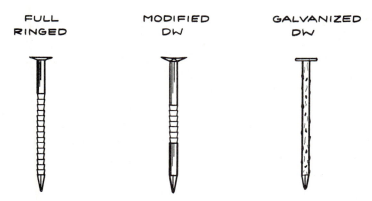

Figure 2-50   Three recognized drywall nails with good holding characteristics.

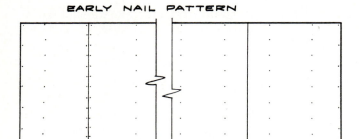

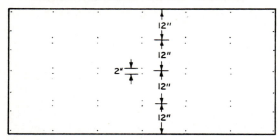

Figure 2-51 These nailing diagrams for walls and ceiling will prove adequate for most conditions provided nails of correct type and length are used and good nailing technique is practiced.

apart. Should a nail fail for any reason, the companion one would do. This formation also has the advantage of reducing the time for compounding over the dimples.

Spacing in the field is generally on 12″-centered pairs. For example, vertically up the 4′-wide board a nail will be placed at 1″; 11 and 13″; 23 and 25″; 35 and 37″; and 47″. There is just one nail at each edge, which is within the cupped area.

Fastening the board to the ceiling, unlike the walls, will benefit from evenly spaced nails because the board is hanging by the nailheads (tension rather than shear stress). Without adhesive, more nails are needed. A nail every 6″ will not be excessive. The factor involved is the quantity of nailhead surface required to support the weight imposed, assuming that the nails will not pull loose from the wood. Too few nails can set up a predisposed failure condition, where first the surface paper gives away around the nailhead, followed by fracture of the gypsum. This is why it is so important to avoid overdimpling (fractured gypsum) or paper cutting from a nonparallel nailhead (slanted nail).

Dimpling a nailhead (Fig. 2-52) is a skill born of dexterity and practice. The process is characteristic of drywalling for the specific purpose of providing a depression for the compounding, the covering up of untaped nails. Dimpling is not a unique experience on drywall, as it occurs repeatedly on structural woodwork. Construction nails are usually given a final blow to sink the head at least flush with the surface and preferably slightly below. There are two significant dissimilarities between frame nailing and drywall nailing. The drywall nail must not cut the paper or crush the gypsum plaster between. To do so is to lose most of the effective holding power on ceiling applications. Wall application is not quite as critical since the wallboard is hanging with shear stress on the nail shanks. The nails on the wall can be compared to so many little hooks.

The second dissimilarity is that drywall nails must be driven as perpendicularly to the surface as possible so that the head is parallel to the surface. Again this is most important on the ceiling because the board depends on the nailheads only for support unless adhesive is used throughout. All nails in the field are nailed straight, at right angles to the surface.

It takes only three or four whacks to successfully put in each nail: one to start it, one to put it flush with the surface, and a final pop shot to dimple it. The first two blows are of the follow-through type. The dimple blow is made like cracking a whip. The downward motion of the hammer is abruptly restricted at the critical movement of impact. It is the same psychomotor response as that called "pulling a punch" in boxing. It takes practice and feeling to develop the skill of dimpling.

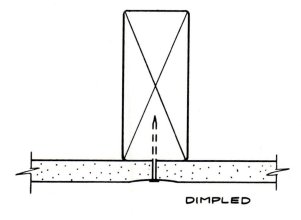

DIMPLED

Figure 2-52 "Dimpling the nail" means sinking the head below the surface with the rounded head of a hammer or DW hatchet without breaking the paper or crushing the gypsum.

Unfortunately, the most difficult and exacting part of the house drywall job comes first, the ceiling. The novice builder usually finds the backhand hammer swing to be the most difficult. The ceiling calls for a lot of backhanding. About the only relief for this problem is to adjust for the height of individuals so that each is at the best possible height in relation to the ceiling surface. Short-legged horses upon which scaffold planks are placed will aid. Whatever the setup, room space is needed for a couple of T bars or a Gyp-C-Jack.

Pressure on the wallboard is required during nailing, whether it is ceiling or wall application (Fig. 2-53). Start the nail; then press the board firmly against the nailing surface with the free hand. Sustain this contact pressure until the nail is dimpled. Failure to follow this practice consistently will result in unseen damage on the back side of the board. A nail that is permitted to pull the board toward the stud or joist breaks the plaster under the paper and frequently goes unnoticed until a future problem erupts.

Rectifying a faulty nail is not difficult. Usually, a new nail can be placed a couple of inches away in undamaged territory. The old spot is simply grouted over with compound. This procedure is advisable wherever a known or suspected weakness in nailing appears.

Checking for high nails needs to be done systematically before starting the tape job. There are two touch methods that work effectively. One can perform the first check subconsciously after it

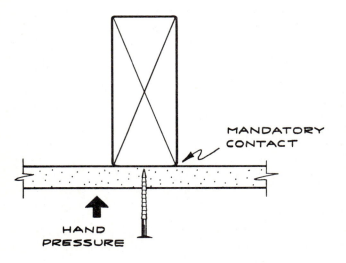

MANDATORY CONTACT

HAND PRESSURE

Figure 2-53 Hold the wallboard tightly against the stud or ceiling joists while driving a nail. Contact must be sustained throughout the nail driving to avoid breaking out the back side of the board and crushing the gypsum around the nail.

becomes a habit. After the dimpling blow, gently slide the head of your hammer across the nailhead. If the head protrudes, a metallic sound will be heard, a clear indicator that the nail needs to be driven a little deeper.

A final overall check can be made with a framing square. Grasp the body at the end. Place the tongue against the wall or ceiling and quickly run it over all the nails in a line. To inspect a ceiling, simply walk along pressing the tongue against a row of nails. The square will make a little snapping sound as it passes over a protruding nail. Stop and sink that nail.

CORNER BEAD

In a typical house, there will be a number of places where drywall goes around a right-angled corner. There are vertical corners on partition ends, jogs in walls, room dividers, recessed bookcases, and openings. Horizontal corners are present in most homes on kitchen soffits. Gypsum board that passes around a corner must be protected from physical damage and given a finished appearance. To achieve these objectives, a sheet metal V-shaped protector is used. It is called a drywall corner bead. After application, compounding and painting, nothing will show to indicate the presence of the metal-protected corner.

Curiously, this corner bead is manufactured in 10' lengths. All vertical corners extending from floor to ceiling in a conventional-height house will require custom cutting of the bead to an appropriate length. The bead should butt the ceiling. On the lower end, some builders will extend the bead almost to the floor. This method will necessitate planing off a portion of the back side of the baseboard. If this is not done, a machine-cut miter joint on the baseboard will stand open. The corner with its buildup of compound and corner bead is not perfectly square. Another builder technique is to permit the baseboard to make the small outward bend over the feathered compound and make the miter cut a little less than 45° to close it. Another technique is to end the metal bead at the top of the baseboard. No compound is permitted below this level.

The problem only presents itself where drywall is full thickness under the corner bead (no cup). The bead metal and nails will all be above the surface line. This cannot be avoided completely.

The problem can be modified a little by using cutoffs from cupped edges of sheets on narrow corners. This works nicely on soffits, archways, and ends of dividers. It keeps at least one side of a corner bead flange below the surface line.

Fitting drywall to an external partition corner (Fig. 2-54) is the easiest form of fitting in the house. Simply choose a sheet long enough to go beyond the corner and nail it in place. Then cut the back side adjacent to the framing by drawing a knife along the corner. Fold it back to a point less than 90°. Run the knife up this crease on the face side. Install the adjacent piece and repeat the process. The resulting corner will be lapped (Fig. 2-55). It presents a desirable solid backing for the corner bead. The method is foolproof in terms of fit and calculation error. A sandboard is used to eliminate any gypsum knobs that protrude above or beyond the surface of the corner, as these will interfere with the seating of the metal corner bead.

Corner bead installing involves the principles of straightness, centering (bisecting the corner angle), and parallelism. One method is to nail the ends first. Press the bead toward the point of the corner. To assure that the corner of the bead bisects the wall corner precisely, each flange must be an identical distance away from the corner. If "eyeballing" does not produce accurate results, a pencil mark can be placed on each side. The flanges are brought

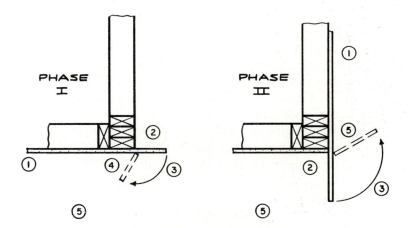

Figure 2-54 An external corner is fitted precisely in a few seconds by following these steps: (1.) Install a board. (2.) Cut the back side with a knife. (3.) Snap the scrap and fold it around. (4.) Cut the crease. (5.) Rasp off the knobs.

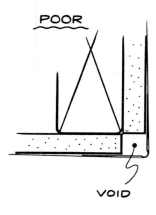

POOR

VOID

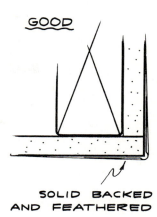

GOOD

SOLID BACKED
AND FEATHERED

Figure 2-55   A lapped corner provides sturdier backing for a corner bead and makes it easier to install the bead.

to the mark or to points equidistant from the marks. Nail the top and bottom first.

The handiest tool to assist in positioning the remainder of the bead straight and true is a 6′ level. Hold the level against the rounded corner of the bead. Apply pressure with both hands held about 3 to 4′ apart. One hand pressing in the middle may bend the level. Ignore the bubbles. This is an exercise in straightness, not plumbness. Plumbness was dealt with at framing time. Note how much movement, if any, is required on each flange side. Set the level aside. Press the bead to the points of reference and place a nail on each side above and below the center of the height. There are two hole sizes on the flanges. One is just large enough for the diameter of a drywall nail. The other is about three times that diameter. Put the two gauge nails into the larger holes. Stagger them apart from each other about 4 to 6″. Sink the nails until the flange is snug to the drywall surface. Recheck the straightness again with the level. If a slight outward bow exists, hold a small wood block over the bead to protect it from denting. Tap the block with your hammer. The bead will move inward. The bead will hold its position if there is enough pressure from the nail heads. Check the straightness again. When the strip is straight, complete the nailing by dividing the distances in half until there is a nail about every 8″ to 12″. Press in or tap out as you go. Finally, check it by holding the straightedge (the level) on the corner of the bead and on each side.

The stud corner post may not be perfectly straight. The manner in which the bead is installed presents the last opportunity to create a straight corner by installing the bead straight. The feathered-out compound will complete the impression of a straight situation. Where two beads complete the end of a divider partition or arch, remember that the two should be perfectly parallel before compounding begins.

A three-surface corner junction (Fig. 2-56) requires some miter cutting of bead ends. Where more than one piece of metal bead is required, a corner or butt joint is necessary. The lower corner of a free-hanging kitchen soffit fits this category. Ends of flanges must not overlap and create too much thickness. On the three-surface corner, the meeting flange ends are mitered back away from the point of intersection about 43°. On straight-run junctions, the flanges on one or the other butting piece are mitered a few degrees so that there is no contact between the flange ends.

The beads should touch at junctions so that a continuous hard corner is presented. Lineup of the beads is difficult but possible

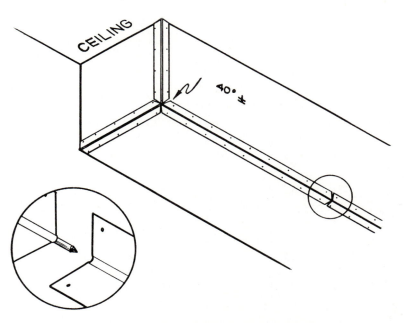

Figure 2-56 Corners of DW bead that meet from three surfaces are mitered a little less than 45° to prevent overlapping metal. Straight junctions that lack solid backing may be pinned with small dowels made from half a nail pinched in the groove.

with no backup. A simple way of providing continuity (a smooth flowthrough) is to use a nail for a dowel pin. Cut the head from a nail of the same diameter as the bead groove. Cut it in half to make two dowels. Slip this little steel dowel half its length down the groove of the first bead that has been installed. Crimp it with pliers if it is loose. Install the next piece over the protruding dowel. Nail the bead in position and then crimp it over the dowel. When nailing at the corner, be mindful of where the wood is that backs up the drywall. Nail only into sound backing.

Bead corners longer than 10′ will benefit from the use of a string line or a chalk line. A chalk line is snapped from the beginning and ending points of the flange edges on both adjacent surfaces of the corner. On a soffit, these are the vertical face and the underside. Set a few nails alternately while pressing the flanges to the chalk lines. Hold a stringline along the bead to check the straightness before completing the nailing. It is important that a soffit be as straight as possible along the lower leading edge. It is here that the junction of cabinets and soffit will be most critical.

COMPOUNDING THE DRYWALL JOINTS

Not everyone will handle the taping and compounding of joints well. It is a highly developed skill. A competent crew of journeymen with adequate tools and machines will put all the tape bedding, tape, and cover coat on a moderate-sized house in a working day. A novice working alone will take weeks to finish a house completely. The cost is a factor to consider. A contract crew may bed tape one day, finish coat another day, and return for a few hours of touch-up sanding on a third day. These are not always consecutive days, as it frequently requires more curing time than overnight. The contract cost for finishing alone is about equal to the cost of the wallboard material. With this knowledge, one has a basis on which to make a decision as to whether one wants to tackle the job or if some alternative wall covering will be considered, such as paneling or wet plaster.

Should one decide to forge ahead, a good first step is to get one steadfast rule firmly embedded. It is: Any compound that goes on and remains on above the wall or ceiling line surface must later be removed the hard way, by sanding. The opposite of this rule, the true fact, is that, properly applied, the compound requires very little sanding to render a flat, paintable surface.

How can one avoid the entrapment of compound buildup? It is simple. Screed. Screed means to scrape off all that which is above the surface. The cupped joint, for example, presents about a 5″-wide trench into which the compound bed, the tape, and the covering coat are initially troweled. Any operator using the hand method of bedding would likely spread and bed with a 3″ or 4″ knife (a wedge-shaped spreader with a handle). To assure that no compound remains above the surface line of the wallboard, however, it will require a 6″ knife that will span across the cupped valley. A 10″ T-shaped knife or a trowel will actually perform the function better.

Perforated tape called Perf-A-Tape is the most economical type in use for covering the cupped joints and inside corners (Fig. 2-57). Tiny holes are burned in this 2″ tape, which permits the bedding compound to penetrate the paper. The bedding side of the tape is fuzzy next to the edges. The design improves the tenacity of the tape. Self-adhesive grid tapes are available but are quite costly by comparison.

Spreading the bedding for tape is tricky (Fig. 2-57). The compound loses its adhesiveness very quickly when exposed to air. The tape must be pressed into the compound within a matter of seconds; otherwise, it will not stick. If embedding is delayed a moment too long, the embedded tape will develop bubbles underneath and peel away from the bed. Only a few feet of tape can be bedded at a time by one person. Usually, about 4′ is the limit. Corner tape should be folded first before pressing it into the compound.

There are two types of machines on the market for tape bedding. One is nicknamed a "banjo," the other a "bazooka," both due to their musical instrument shape. The banjo taper is basically a box dispenser that permits rolling the tape through wet compound before it is placed. The bazooka is a long tube and roller that facilitates taping the ceiling joints from floor level. Both machines incorporate the same principle, to put the tape and compound on simultaneously. In many areas these machines can be rented. It is a good investment in time and callback insurance. Without an automatic taper, the next best system is to involve a partner or two. The lead-off person spreads the bed, the second person presses in the tape, and the third person covers it immediately and screeds it flush. From there on it can be a one-person completion job.

Shadow testing is a method of identifying high and low spots of compound. The creamy manila color of compound makes it

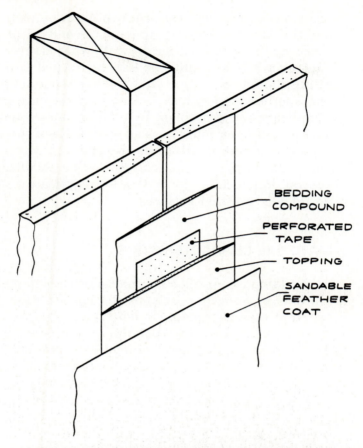

Figure 2-57 Drywall joint finishing is a three-stage operation: (1.) Bed the tape in compound and cover it with a screeded coat. (2.) Apply a finish coat and feather out the edges. (3.) Remove high spots and small, trowel-formed ridges with a sand board.

difficult by sight alone to see rolls and depressions. Such slight malformations can frequently be identified better with the sense of feel in the hands than by sight. A true gauge of the contours is a straightedge backed by a light source. The straightedge must be long enough to bridge the compounded area. A 10″ trowel will serve well for most of the cupped joints. A framing square body (the 24″ leg) is adequate for larger feathered spans.

Hold the straightedge nearly perpendicular to the surface. Draw it slowly along the compounded joint or area. Hold a trouble light or flashlight behind the straightedge as it is moved along. Depressions will show up as cracks of light between the straightedge and the surface. Actually, unless both ends of the straightedge are touching the surface of the drywall, what is revealed is a high spot. Wherever the straightedge can be rocked from end to end, no filling should take place until the high spot(s) has been sanded off and another shadow test performed. There is a great possibility of complicating the problem by adding more compound to "smooth out" a rolling or roughness situation. Keep the important rule of thumb in mind at all times. *No excess compound should be left above the surface of the wallboard line.* Adding compound when subtracting is called for will only complicate a solution or lead to an uneven finished surface.

MATERIAL CHARACTERISTICS

All building materials have characteristics that affect such considerations as when to purchase, storage life, how to store, where to use, and how to protect for long life. Gypsum products, properly chosen and applied, are a popular and satisfactory product for residential construction use. Some of the manufacturers' listed products and uses are the following: Board thicknesses include ⅝, ½, ⅜ and ¼". A single layer of ⅝" drywall provides a strong wall surface with increased resistance to fire. It is used extensively in commercial applications. Single-layer, ½"-thick drywall is currently a universal residential system for wall covering; ⅜" is used in the double system of layering and for overlaying on a remodeling job; ¼"-thick sheets are used as an underlayment for ¼" paneling and for overlay remodeling.

W/R (water resistant) drywall is characterized by its green paper covering. It is the only type of gypsum-based wallboard recommended for interior locations exposed to dampness. Regular drywall (cream-colored paper) should never be used as a base under bathroom tile or adhesive-bonded plastic-coated hardboard. The gypsum core of W/R is protected with an asphalt emulsion. Even so, cut edges or exposed edges should be further sealed with a specially formulated W/R sealant.

Store drywall sheets flat and out of the weather. When stored in the house, one should keep in mind the great weight involved. A stack of drywall 2' or 3' high will put a tremendous strain on floor joists, especially when the stack is in the middle of the span. An attached garage with a concrete floor is a good place for drywall awaiting installation. Plywood sheets laid under the stack will help prevent the first few sheets from absorbing moisture from the slab (Fig. 2-58). Due to the vulnerability of drywall to damage, it should be brought to the job site only when it is time for it to be installed.

Drywall comes packaged two sheets to a pack. Each end of the pack is held together with a heavy paper tape strip. To transport one sheet at a time, first grasp the end of the tape and sharply pull away. It will tear off neatly all the way across. Repeat on the other end. The finish face sides of the two sheets lie in the pack touching each other. Do not grasp the end of the top sheet of a fresh pack and slide it across the lower sheet in the pack. Any small grain of sand or plaster that is trapped between the sheets will roll or drag, leaving an indented track that later requires compounding. Occasionally, a little curl of torn surface paper will develop. The resulting damage is difficult to repair with compound. The damage may require discarding or downgrading the sheet.

Compound is available in powder form and in ready-mixed, all-purpose form. The key to which form one should choose lies mainly in the quantity and expertise of the appliers. One person

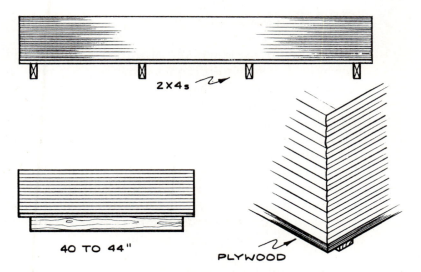

Figure 2-58   Twelve packs (24 sheets) of drywall stacked neatly on an unassembled pallet of plywood and scrap 2 × 4. This gypsum board should be in good condition when ready to use.

working with hand tools will not apply compound fast enough to warrant a large container of ready-mix. The frequent opening and closing of the container will render the last portion useless. Compound deteriorates over a period of time. It glazes over and dries out rapidly when exposed. It loses its adhesion quality for tape bedding. Purchase only in quantities that can be used up within a few days. Storage over longer periods may prove fruitless.

In powder form, there are different types of compound for different purposes. A type for tape bedding has superior adhesion qualities. A top-coating type is designed to sand more easily. All-purpose compounds simplify inventory and prevent possible use of the wrong kind. Some loss of superior adhesion and surface quality is sacrificed in the trade-off. All three types should be brought to room temperature before application or mixing begins.

For those with an interest in obtaining more information on the detail and scope of drywall, an excellent reference is the *Gypsum Construction Handbook*, published by the United States Gypsum Company, 101 South Wacker Drive, Chicago, IL, 60606. The price is nominal and will be quoted by the company on request. It is an authoritative handbook and well worth the small investment.

9 PANELING

The patterning and cutting of wall paneling is similar to that of drywall. A notable difference, however, is found in the finishing media. The basic finishing medium for drywall is compound. It is fluid in nature. This fluid characteristic couples neatly with the nature of drywall edges to be easily damaged. This provides an application method that allows the installer to intentionally cut a drywall sheet short to assure that it will fit on the first try without breaking corners and edges. The fluid filler takes care of the gaps.

Fluid fillers for paneling are seldom used, with the exception of small repairs. The system for covering corners is either to mate the two adjoining edges perfectly or to cover an internal or external corner with a piece of molding (Fig. 2-59).

Edge joining of sheets on a common surface may also be done by tight fitting or by covering with a coordinated strip. The thickness of the paneling and the material will dictate the finishing system to some extent. For example, three-ply, ¼″-thick

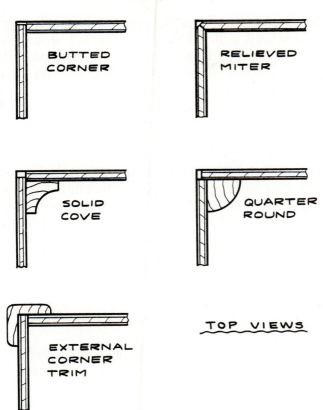

BUTTED
CORNER

RELIEVED
MITER

SOLID
COVE

QUARTER
ROUND

EXTERNAL
CORNER
TRIM

TOP VIEWS

Figure 2-59   Internal paneled
corners that are fitted without
trim. Internal corners with trim.
External paneled corner with
wood trim.

hardwood paneling that is basically stiff can be butt joined at the
edges effectively. Three-mil-thick imported panels of soft wood,
such as Luan mahogany, usually must be glued to any
underlayment and frequently covered at the joints to eliminate
rippling. Although Luan and some other forms of mahogany are
classed as hardwood, they are soft and pliable by nature.

Other forms of paneling use various cores and backings
that have characteristics with which the builder must be familiar.
Compressed and glued sawdust is a common backing material for
less costly paneling. A photographic vinyl overlay gives an impression of real wood. Indeed, the panel for the most part *is* wood, but it
is totally devoid of grain. Much like drywall, it is prone to corner
damage. Grasped in the wrong place and flexed a little too much,
this particle board panel frequently breaks in half. Nonetheless,
with proper handling, adequate adhesive installation, and quality
trimming, a good-looking job can be had.

Hardboard is another common backing material for synthetic paneling. It is strong and durable in a surface structural sense. Wood-grained photographic decal surfaces as well as wallpaper and fabrics are available on hardboard backing. The trade name Masonite is frequently associated with hardboard.

Cost consideration will require an analysis of all the materials required to install a particular type of paneling. Consider these principles. The thinner panels may require costly cover and joint trim. Corner coves and surrounds are sold by the piece or by the linear foot. When quoted as 12, 17, or 23 cents a foot, it does not sound like much. It could end up costing as much for the extra time and adhesive as for the thin paneling itself. At first glance, a good-looking piece of paneling at one-third the cost of another seems like a good deal. Have a closer look and then make a decision based on all the facts at hand.

PANEL LAYOUT

Paneling is usually left until after the installation of a hardwood floor or of underlayment. It is explained here due to its similarities to gypsum board.

Layout of the paneling is done in accordance with the finish carpenter's philosophy. It is usually better to make the piece a little large and be able to trim it than to make it what seems to be dimensionally correct only to find it is too small. It is a mistake to assume that, because the panel is square, the area for which it is being customized will also be square.

Whether a pattern is laid out on the face or the back of a panel may depend on the type of saw being used and/or the size of the teeth. A circular saw and saber saw (portable jigsaw) should be operated on the back side of paneling or plywood as less surface splintering will thus occur. The teeth on these saws tear the most on the side of the material where they exit the cut. The chipping takes place on the top side with a saber saw or a hand-operated skill saw. Chipping can be minimized somewhat with finer-toothed blades, but a sacrifice in cutting time will result. A handsaw, table saw, or bandsaw chips on the underside where the teeth exit the material. Fine teeth are recommended for panel cutting. A handsaw should have no fewer than 10 points per inch (a number 10 crosscut).

Getting started squarely on each wall will not necessarily occur simply by pressing the first sheet into the corner of the room. A room condition that is not perfectly square, straight, plumb, and level will require careful assessment before placing the lead-off panel. In this situation, parallelism may be more important than plumbness. Striated paneling (vertical grooves) can produce some weird effects if the grooves are not parallel with doors, windows, and room corners. Where these three "vertical" reference lines are not parallel, a compromise will be necessary. Line up the paneling parallel with the reference lines in the room that most dominate the sight impression. For example, the door casings will be very noticeable alongside a dark groove in the paneling unless the groove and casing are parallel. Nonparallel situations will give the impression of an unsquare door opening or a room that is actually tilted. A badly out of square room may be adequate justification to avoid paneling with vertical grooves and choose paneling that does not contain a lot of vertical lines.

Checking for squareness and parallelism can be done by measurement and by testing with a long level. Hold the level vertically against the key places: corner, door jamb, and other openings. Compare plumbness. Next, measure between suspected unparallel edges, where several reference points check plumb and one does not. Probably the logical compromise is to align the paneling with the majority. Remember that every upright reference in the room can be parallel and still not be plumb (they may all tilt in the same direction). This happens where a frame is inadequately braced before sheathing. Another consideration is the length of the upright reference. For example, a corner is the longest reference taken vertically. A door is likely to be next, and windows that do not extend to the floor would come last. Consider also that the vertical jambs on a window are frequently obscured by curtains and a priority rationale emerges. It will be more important to align panel grooves with doors and corners than with windows. In the case of too many misaligned reference points, a panel with highly figured wood grain with few or no vertical lines will do the best job of disguising the unsquareness of the room. The remodeler who is faced with a house that has settled or was built before modular materials were used will benefit from learning well how to assess the conditions in a room before choosing or beginning to install paneling.

Pattern reversal is such a common and repeated problem that it warrants continual reminders. Remember that laying out a pattern on the back side of a panel will always reverse the direction of L and U shapes and the location of openings, such as electric boxes. This assumes that the top and bottom references are not mixed up.

There are situations, such as those involving grain configuration, where a panel mates better to the last one installed by placing a certain edge adjacent. In this case, the panel will have a specific top and bottom relationship. Hold the panel in place to make the determination. Then revolve the panel 180° horizontally while still in an upright position. Mark the back side UP, TOP, or with an arrow before laying it down to draw the pattern on it.

Index wherever possible. It is always more foolproof to put the panel in place and index openings and cuts than to transfer measurements. Reach behind the panel with your trusty red crayon and X mark or circle the general area where a duplex outlet is to be patterned.

Marking electric box cutouts can be frustrating. Paneling cannot be patched as readily as drywall, especially if cut in completely the wrong place. Some helpful hints may help avoid that tragic experience. Follow these simple steps:

1. Hold the panel in position.
2. Reach behind and index the box location.
3. Measure from the closest vertical reference (the room corner if it is the first panel, the adjoining sheet edge from then on) to the edges of the electric box.
4. Measure from the ceiling down to the top of the box, not from the floor.
5. Transfer these measurements to the panel back.
6. Trace an electric box of the same size below the tall measurement and on the proper side of the edge distance mark. Remember, if you turned the panel around, all is reversed except the height.
7. Cut out a plug that is ¼″ smaller than the outline all around.
8. Hold the panel in place off the floor against the ceiling and against the room corner or adjoining panel.
9. Check the hole against the box. Re-mark it if it needs adjustment.
10. Finish cut it.

Index window and door locations onto a panel with the panel propped up in position. More often that not, the edge of a panel will terminate somewhere within the window or door location. This provides the opportunity of reaching behind and tracing the cutout. This is the most foolproof method available. Pattern layout should resort to a transfer of measurements only when no other indexing method is present.

CUTTING THE PANEL

Most panel cutting will take place on sawhorses with supporting 2×4s underneath. The following rules apply:

1. Support the panel adequately so that no pieces break away, causing damage.
2. Arrange supporting 2×4s so that cuts go between them, not over them.
3. Protect the surface of a panel that is facing down from damage from its supports. Protect the surface of a panel that is facing up by putting protective tape on the saw base or the panel.

Do not saw beyond an inside corner with a circular saw. Stop at the corner, or short of the corner, and complete the cut with a handsaw or saber saw. A practical team of power tools for panel cutting is a small circular saw with a 4 or 4½″ blade diameter for medium to long straight cuts and a saber saw for pocket cutting, such as duplex and switch-box openings. The circular saw blade with the front of its baseplate against the surface is pressed down into the wood at each side of the box opening and retracted. The saber is inserted in the kerf to complete the cutout.

ATTACHING PANELS

Generally, panels of ¼″ thickness or more are nailed to the studs through the backing. Thin panels are glued to the gypsum backboard. This is not intended as a rule. The rule is to do what is required to assure that the panels will stay in place as intended. This may involve a combination of nails and adhesives throughout.

With overall adhesive, a few nails may be used in strategic places only.

Panel stiffness is a key element that influences the method of installation. Stiff panels can usually be installed with either nails or adhesive. Adhesive is the material to use where no exposed nailheads are desired. Nails are more certain where conditions of dampness or extreme heat may cause an adhesive to fail.

Thin panels will usually require adhesive throughout and possibly some nails to hold down rebellious curves and bubbles. Some thin panels seem stiff enough to install fairly well without overall adhesive contact, but later succumb to blistering and edge rippling due to swelling. Swollen areas between studs are nearly impossible to rectify after installation—another argument for doing it right in the beginning.

Adhesive may be spread in a variety of patterns. Follow the manufacturer's recommendation if it comes with the panels or with the adhesive (Fig. 2-60). In the absence of such information, a grid system may be followed. A bead of adhesive is spread on the wall surface both vertically and horizontally on 6″ to 8″ spacing intervals. When the panel is pressed into the adhesive, a little pad of adhesive spreads out at the grid intersections. A bead of adhesive

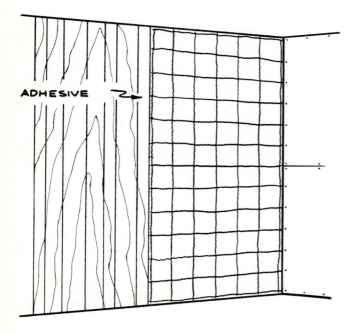

ADHESIVE

Figure 2-60 Adhesive beads in a grid pattern will hold many kinds of paneling to a wall surface successfully.

should always be spread around the perimeter. Experience will tell how far in from the edge to place the bead so that it will not press out beyond the edge when pressure is applied. Pressure must be applied all over the sheet until adhesion takes place. Where a nailed-on baseboard is to be applied later, the panel can be nailed below the top of the baseboard line with 4d nails. These nails, which have larger heads than panel nails, can also be used along the top of the sheet if a corner mold will later be installed to cover them up.

Panel nails come in two standard lengths. The short ones are about 1″ long, the longer ones about 1½″. The annular rings give the little panel nail great holding power. The heads are small, but flat on both sides, to give adequate pull-through protection. The length of nail needed depends on the panel thickness, how much backer thickness exists, and the holding quality of the wood behind the backing wallboard. In some localities, special-purpose gypsum backer board is available with gray paper on both sides and square edges (no cups) at less cost than regular drywall. Drywall backer, regardless of kind, does not provide adequate holding power for any type of nail. Nails should always be placed to reach into wood, a stud or plate.

Coordinating grooves in panels to fall over studs takes planning and forethought. Studs must be located accurately so that every vertical butt joint of the edges of panels will fall precisely centered over a stud. When the edges are accurately aligned, the grooves will automatically be over studs, as they have been designed that way. The backlash from this design is that if the edge of a panel is misplaced (not over a stud), all the grooves will be off. This alignment is important because the proper and least noticeable location to put an exposed nail in the field of the sheet is in a groove. The exception is the thin sheet, where grooves reduce the thickness to a point of uselessness for nailing. In such a case, nails should be staggered from side to side along the groove, and/or this paneling should be glued.

Placing the first sheet into an exterior wall corner usually requires cutting off 4″ or more of the panel width. Such will be the case with a modularly designed house with 2 × 4 frame walls. Say, for example, that the framework is on the building line. The corner post built up of 2 × 4 studs will subtract 3½″ of the 48″ distance to the center of the stud that is on the 4′ major module. Another ½″ is subtracted for the drywall backup board on the adjacent wall. Any variation will affect this formula, such as an exterior wall frame that is inset on the box floor to provide flush-mounted sheathing.

Indexing the actual stud location is a more positive way of dealing with the placement of the first sheet of paneling. The nails holding on the backing board will show the approximate location of the stud. Although every nail in the gypsum board may have hit the stud, few, if any, will be dead centered. Hold the edge of a long level through the center of the greatest quantity of nailheads that can be bisected. Draw this center line vertically starting about 4″ above the floor over the stud where the edge of the first panel edge will be positioned. A couple of inches above the floor drive a 4d nail through the drywall ¾″ right or left of the center line. If it touches wood, move away from the center line ⅛″ and drive it through again. Do the same on the other side of the center line until a clear 1½″-wide x-ray profile of the stud location is established. Repeat this probing procedure 3″ down from the ceiling. Nailing above that level will risk hitting the top plate. This probing should take place on the stud that will receive the edge of the panel, usually the third stud (not counting the corner).

Patterning the first sheet is now possible by measuring horizontally to the corner from the center of each probed area. Should these two measurements vary substantially, it will indicate the presence of an out-of-plumb corner or field stud. Assessment and adaptation must follow. Find out first how plumb the corner is. Adapt the panel's vertical orientation in accordance with the principles of parallelism to other dominant features of the room, as described a few paragraphs earlier. It may develop that the lead edge of the panel will of necessity be diagonal across the stud from top to bottom. If such is the case, see to it that the panel edge passes through the center of the stud at a point halfway up the height of the wall. This will assure the best nailing base that can be achieved without canting (tilting) the panel unduly.

Press the top of the sheet up to the ceiling with the edge in the corner and nail it. If the wall exceeds the panel height, it will be better to have the gap at the bottom behind a wide baseboard than at the top behind a narrower cove molding. In the unsquare situation, let only the high corner of the panel touch the ceiling. Occasionally, the unsquareness is such that a panel cannot be placed without trimming. Trim it at the top. Trim it so that the top edge more closely fits or partially parallels the ceiling. The top and bottom are usually covered. Precise fit here is not necessary. Precise junctions of the edges *are* required.

Start nailing at the center of a panel and work out. This is a good rule, but sometimes it is necessary to place a few nails along the edge to prevent the panel from shifting while field nailing progresses. Nail spacing is optional, depending on panel stiffness and how well the nails are holding. Six to eight or sometimes ten to twelve inches will prove adequate in the field. The vertical edges will require more. Put enough 4d regular nails (coated are best) along top and bottom to assure that there will be no ripples under the cove and baseboard. A considerable savings can be realized by using these nails in hidden places (under molding). Their cost is only a fraction of panel nail cost. No closer spacing is required around windows and doors than in the field, as these areas are effectively held down by the casing or corner mold that will cover them later.

Dealing with nail color is something to be considered. Standard colors that are available in panel nails are black, white, tan, and brown. Others are made for specific panels. For surface nailing, obtain and use the color that most closely blends with the color of the panel. Many panels have grooves that are a darker color than the panel. Match the nail color to the groove as much as possible. Where a close match is not possible, use lighter nails on light panels and darker nails on dark panels. The contrast will not appear as great.

The vertical edges of a grooved panel have a half-groove. Frequently, this half-groove is not wide enough or thick enough to be nailed. Nails will have to be placed on the panel surface close to the half-groove. Stay within ¼″ of the groove so that each nail can be driven straight and will hit the stud. Choose a nail color that blends well with the surface of the paneling.

Set each nailhead flush with the surface wherever possible. It will punch its own countersink. Avoid using a nailset. A nailset has a tendency to chip off the color coating on the head of the nail. It is also very easy to slip off the hardened nailhead and punch an unsightly hole alongside. A pop action on the final blow, as described for dimpling a drywall nail, will produce a flush-set head. Avoid slanting any nails, as the head will then fracture a half-moon cut in the veneer of the panel and leave an unsightly depression. All exposed nailheads should be left flush with the surface and smooth to the touch for dusting and waxing efficiency.

DRYWALL PANEL BACKING

A unique problem (which is seldom thought of until too late) exists with dark-grooved panels placed over drywall backing. The light-colored gypsum board backing will show through any joint that is not compressed very tightly. The slightest amount of panel shrinkage or shifting will expose this sliver of light. The tiniest slippage during nailing will cause it. A preventive solution is to darken the area behind the edge junction of the panels (Fig. 2-61). Many materials for darkening will do. An aerosol can of black paint can be used to spray a strip up or down behind the junction areas. A panel can be nailed onto three studs first, leaving the leading edge unnailed. A black felt-tipped marker is then run down the area while holding up the edge of the panel. If one forgets and nails the

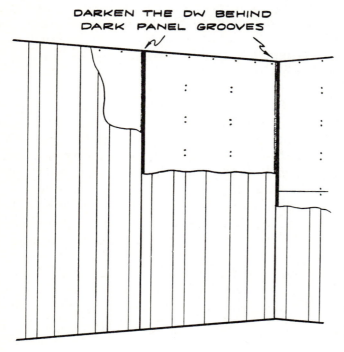

Figure 2-61 The area behind a panel joint should be darkened when medium to dark paneling is installed so that there is no chance of the light-colored backerboard showing through.

edge of the panel, the marker can be pressed into the corner of the edge and firmly run down the backing board. The fluid in the marker will spread under the edge a little. Dark oil stain applied with a small brush will produce the same result. Dark brown or black crayons will make a lasting mark. Black crepe paper or plastic film can be cut in 2″ strips and stapled at top and bottom to mask the area. Whatever the method, it will be worth remembering to eliminate a pesky problem before it occurs.

MOLDINGS

Applying molding to "trim out" the paneling may be a labor of love or a nasty frustration. Any tool or machine that will cut a 45° miter will simplify and speed the job. For external corners, the casing or molding is mitered. (Fig. 2-62). No end grain will show when the mating cuts are made correctly. Molding that meets at an internal corner may be mitered or coped. To cope means to cut a mating contoured profile on the end of molding. Molding around the top of the wall at the ceiling junction is called *crown mold*, as it resembles the crown mold on the exterior of some period homes. Smaller molds are called *bed mold*.

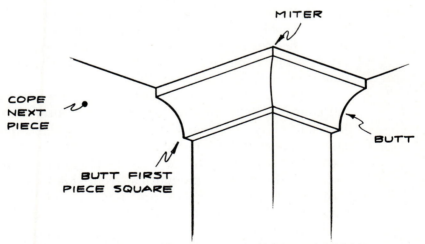

Figure 2-62 The internal corners at the ceiling line are trimmed with cove or crown molding. Internal corner pieces are butted and coped. External corners are mitered.

Crown mold is obtainable in many shapes and sizes. It is usually installed first. An objective is to cause the grain of the molding and the contours to flow uninterrupted around internal and external corners without exposing any end grain or losing the profile of the pattern. To achieve this objective, the external corners are surrounded by molding ends that are mitered (cut at a 45° angle to go around a 90° corner).

Internal corners may be trimmed in the same manner by mitering the molding. A problem frequently develops with a mitered internal corner joint. Shrinkage occurs and the two intersecting molds move apart, causing a gap. Unless the ends of the miters are stained or painted before installation, the gap will expose bare wood, which often contrasts with the color of the stained surface. This condition can largely be avoided by cutting the end of one piece of the mold to match the contour of the other. This is called coping because it was done with coping saws before the existence of so many power tools. Also, it produces a coping pattern in reverse. *Coping* is a general term for fancy trim around the top of a building. Most wall-to-ceiling junctions will be crowned with a concave-shaped molding called *cove*.

Installing the first piece of cove is simplest because both ends are cut square when a single piece will span the full length or width of a room. The back corner of each square-cut piece usually requires a little chamfering with a pocket knife to mate with the compounded drywall corner. From there on, one end of the molding will be coped to mate with the face of the square-ended preceding piece at the corner of the room. It will be cut square on the lead end where it butts the next corner of the room. The last pieces require coping on both ends.

Where a cove molding piece is not long enough to reach the full length of the room, the leading end is mitered at a 45° angle to form half of a scarf joint (Fig. 2-63). This is the same lap-type joint used on the cove facia board outside. There is a remarkable difference when setting up to cut a cove scarf joint. A cove that is symmetrical (the pattern is identical from side to side) can easily be revolved in the miter box and end up not fitting its partner. Square-cut butt joints should never be used, as the slightest shrinkage will open up the joint to the same problems as those described for the internal miter joint. Ceiling cove must be situated in the miter saw or radial saw with the back side against the fence and its lower edge on the table, the same position as found on the wall.

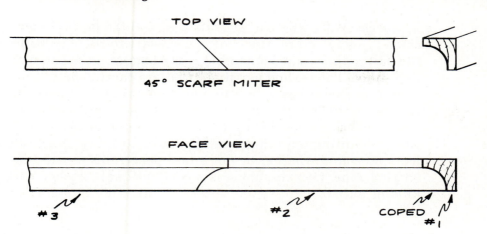

TOP VIEW

45° SCARF MITER

FACE VIEW

#3   #2   COPED
                              #1

Figure 2-63   Joints between corners of this small cove are scarf cut at 45°. Installation order is numbered 1, 2, 3.

External corners are always mitered to prevent the exposure of end grain. It is advisable to cut the piece a minute amount long. When installing the first piece that will go around an external corner, have a short piece with a mitered complementary end at hand to hold in place as a gauge. The gauge miter is held against the miter of the piece to be nailed. It will show precisely how far the first mold should extend beyond the corner. Do not try to eyeball the hangover of the first piece by sighting the inside of the miter with the corner. It will almost always cause the miter to fall short of its required position.

Spread glue on the mitered surfaces as each piece is fitted. Do not wipe off any excess that squeezes out the corner. It will seal the surface grain and prevent stain from penetrating. Come back later and peel off the slightly hardened glue. The glue may be wiped off immediately from trim that will be painted.

Lock the joint with two small finish nails, one from each side. The little barbed panel nails are also excellent joint holders if they can be driven parallel enough with the grain and still present a head fairly square with the curved surface of the cove.

Nailing the cove is a particular job. Small coves are solid throughout. Larger sizes are usually hollow on the back side. A triangular void will exist behind the larger cove mold. One might subconsciously think that a nail driven at a 45° angle centered in the face of the cove would draw it snugly into the corner. On exterior walls and partitions perpendicular to ceiling joists, such will be the case only where a nail hits a joist. If the joists cannot be located reliably and routinely, it is necessary to change the angle of the nail so that it anchors in the upper plate. On the end walls of a gable-roofed house and partitions that are parallel to ceiling joists, a ceiling backer board will provide anchoring for the cove nails. Consciously attempt to x-ray visualize the locality of solid wood into which each nail can anchor. A sense of "feel" is important when mounting anything over gypsum board. One must sense by feel and sound whether or not a nail penetrates an adequate anchoring zone. Gypsum alone is not an adequate anchor with any kind of nail.

DOOR CASING

Casing the doors will phase into the trimming sequence in relation to the junction made between the casing and paneling. There are three alternatives resulting from the manner of panel fitting.

1. Install the paneling before the door jambs are installed (Fig. 2-64). With ½″ drywall backing and ¼″ paneling, the jamb depth of an interior passage will be the same as for the wet

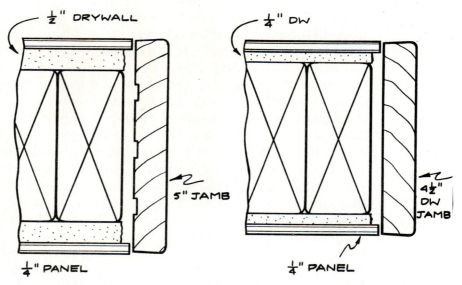

Figure 2-64 Various combinations of backerboard and panel thickness can be used to match stock jamb widths.

plaster system (⅜″ lath and ⅜″ wet plaster on each side plus 3½″ of stud equals 5″). One-half inch drywall plus ¼″ panel on each side plus the 3½″ stud also equals 5″. With this combination, the same-depth jamb will be ordered. Another possible combination (economy alternative) is 3-mil paneling with ⅜″ drywall backing, which combines nicely with the standard drywall jamb (4½″ depth). Three-mil panel is ever so slightly over ⅛″ thick. Another alternative is ¼″ panel over ¼″ drywall to match the drywall module jamb. In all these combinations, the paneling is traced in place to the rough openings in the same way that the drywall was and cut. It can usually be nailed in place and cut out in similar fashion if desired.

2. Install the door jambs before the paneling. Omit the casing. Temporarily tack the panel or have someone hold it in place over the door opening. Trace the required cutout. Cut parallel to but far enough away from the lines to accommodate the thickness of the jamb. About ⅛″ more than the thickness away will make fitting easier. A precise fit is unnecessary, as the casing will cover the area completely. Installation of jambs and casing is explained a little later.

3. Install drywall jambs less the casing. Hold or temporarily tack casing in place. Trace around the casing onto the drywall with a sharp pencil. Remove the casing. Cut a rabbet in the

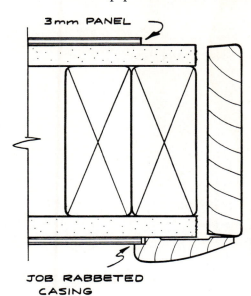

3mm PANEL

JOB RABBETED CASING

Figure 2-65 A technique for accommodating 3-mm paneling with stock jambs is to rabbet the casing. This method also works well for remodeling jobs.

back outer edge of the casing that is as deep as the thickness of the panel and out ¼ to ⅜″ across the casing. The rabbet can be machined on a jointer, a table saw, or a shaper or can be cut with a router. The panel is then cut to pattern so that it will be under the rabbeted edge of the casing (Fig. 2-65). This is a good method of holding down the edges of thin panels that tend to bulge between nails. It is also a good method for retrofit jobs where replacement of jambs is not warranted.

A poor alternative of joining a panel to a casement is to butt the junction. It is possible, but so meticulous and time consuming as to be unreasonable for the one-time builder and nonfeasible for the professional trimmer.

BASEBOARD AND BASE SHOE

Baseboard and base shoe are next in the trimming sequence after door casing is completed and floor underlayment or hardwood floor is laid, whether it be a wetwall, drywall, or paneled wall skin. Two common baseboard designs are popular and available at most suppliers (Fig. 2-66). One is the streamlined type that gently curves from a ⅛″ flat top outward and down to a bottom about ½″ thick. The other is the pattern casing. The back side is hollowed out on

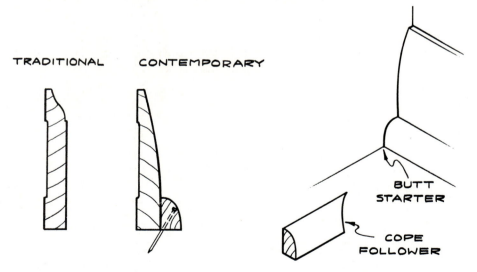

TRADITIONAL   CONTEMPORARY

BUTT STARTER

COPE FOLLOWER

Figure 2-66 Baseboard and base shoe are butted and coped in the same manner as crown coping.

both styles throughout the central section to make it easier to pull the edges tight to the wall surface. For this reason, finish nails should only be placed along the top and bottom, and not over the hollow-backed area. Use nails long enough to bridge the drywall (and paneling), which will penetrate the soleplate or stud at least ¾″. Since the top of the baseboard is thinner, the nail used there will be a size smaller than the one used at the bottom.

Butting the baseboard to a door casing is a simple matter of cutting the baseboard square where the door mold style is a little thicker than the baseboard. Where the two molds are the same thickness, the end of the baseboard will require a little rounding over on the face to make it appear finished.

Internal and external baseboard and base shoe corner junctions are handled the same as crown molding junctions. A machine method of indicating the pattern to follow can be effectively established by vertically mitering the end of the board first (Fig. 2-67). A coping saw is then used to cut along the contour where the miter

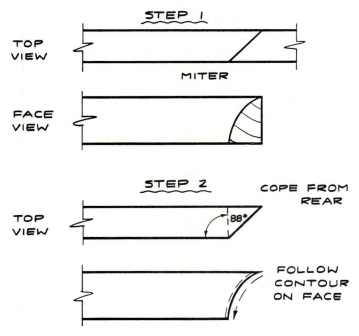

Figure 2-67 Patterning a coping cut can be done by first making a vertical 45° miter. Next, cut the cope from the back vertical side following the contour line made by the miter on the face. Undercut a few degrees so the face contour touches tightly on adjacent piece.

cut severed the face. Undercut the pattern slightly less than 90° to the face. This will permit the face edge of the coped end to fit tightly against the face of the adjoining baseboard in the corner.

Base shoe is a smaller piece of rounded molding placed against the floor and baseboard. The upper edge is rounded to shed dust. The purpose of the base shoe is to form a seal between the flooring and the baseboard. It is common for the wood materials in the floor and wall to shrink a little. A crack often develops at the bottom of the baseboard. The base shoe is nailed in a bedding compression mode so that the bottom and back press equally against the floor and the wall. To accomplish this objective, each nail is driven diagonally through the surface at approximately a 45° angle. The nail is not intended to go through the baseboard; however, it is difficult to miss it and still pull the shoe tight to the surface. The ½″-thick base shoe is not sturdy enough to permit the use of large, long finish nails that will reach the sole or floor sheathing. Solid wood backing like the wet-plaster grounding board of wet-wall days is no longer used. With drywall there is no need for the screed guide (plaster ground board). The popularity of wall-to-wall carpeting has reduced the need to use base shoe. There is no reason for expensive hardwood flooring to be laid under wall-to-wall carpeting. Many consumers prefer to put their money into long-lasting quality carpeting instead of hardwood flooring that would be completely covered. As a result of this evolution, the function and use of base shoe have substantially disappeared, although it is still used where hardwood floors are prescribed.

CORNER TRIMMING

Vertical corner trimming comes next in the paneling sequence. Internal corners may be trimmed with a molding or the panels may be carefully fitted (mated) so that no molding is required. A cove-shaped molding has a small advantage over a convex quarter-round pattern. The cove with its concave pattern will butt the ceiling cove and the baseboard edges with less overhanging surface. A small corner cove may therefore be cut square on each end. It will blend fairly well even though the junction is not in perfect unity. For cover-up purposes, use the smallest cove or quarter-round obtainable for the internal corner.

External wood corner mold for paneling is shaped in its cross section like an angle iron. Several sizes are available.

Wooden corner mold of this shape is delicate and easily breakable in transit or storage. If stepped on, it will most certainly crack lengthwise. It is also vulnerable when being installed. A hammer blow too close to the corner may crack the grain. This L-shaped molding may be used around rectangular archways, windows with paneled casements (paneled rough opening), and the end of open partitions (divider walls). Aesthetics or necessity may dictate the choice. Wide pieces are needed to cover poorer panel junctions. Wide corner mold is easier to nail. Nails places close to the outer edges can be driven straight and will hit solid wood backing. Narrow corner mold will require some angling to hit solid wood, as the first ½″ of the corner behind is gypsum. Why not put nails diagonally throughout the joint of the corner mold? It is possible, but a large quantity of breakage may result. Just one too many blows or too hard a final blow will break the mold. Careful side nailing is preferred. Remember that retrofit paneling over old drywall will usually mean nailing through hidden metal corner bead. The resistance will be felt when the nail first contacts the flange. A pop-type blow is needed to puncture the metal without bending the nail. Once punctured, normal delicate hammering may proceed. It is all but impossible to nail directly into the corner of a hidden drywall corner bead in the retrofit situation. The nail will simply veer off to left or right and enter the cavity between the panel and drywall. No holding power results. Corner nailing of wood corner trim *is* possible and can be done successfully where no metal bead is hidden below. Follow these precautions.

1. Be certain that the corner board is not twisted. Start a nail at the top and the bottom to assure its straightness and stress-free contact throughout.

2. Use a nailset as soon as the nailhead is close to the wood surface. Do not hit the wood with the hammer head.

3. Use long, ring-shank panel nails. Sink each head with the nailset just enough to hold putty filler. The wood is too thin for successful use of cup-head finish nails. Their heads are too far through the board after setting to have adequate holding quality.

4. Do not nail closer than 16″ apart. Once attached, the board is quite stiff due to its angle-iron shape. It does not take a lot of nails to hold it in place.

Paneled corners without corner mold will be mitered. Whether or not this mode of finishing is feasible is partly dependent on the thickness and material characteristics of the paneling. The mitered corner will be comparatively sharp and vulnerable to damage. Fuzzy-grained wood will continually present the threat of slivers and splintering. The mitering option on an external corner seldom warrants the time loss. An internal corner, however, can be fitted rapidly with a butt joint.

An alternative to wood-trimmed corners is to use one of many synthetic moldings that are available. Some are shaped like wood cove and have molded grain. Others are shaped with flanges and pockets so that no exposed nails are required. Internal corners of this type may be installed with adhesive with no danger of failure. Whatever the trimming method or material decided on, it is important to look on the paneling and trimming project as a total, integrated process and consider all facets at the outset, especially where cost is important.

10 UNDERLAYMENT FLOORING

Particle board is a modularly shaped sheet of fabricated material. It is comprised of pressure-glued small chips of wood and sawdust. It is dense and fairly stable when kept dry. In $4' \times 8'$ sheets, it is readily obtainable and 100 percent usable. Its moderate cost and ease of installation have made particle board the standard of the industry for a carpet underlayment surface.

The sequence of underlayment installation is optional but somewhat influenced by wall and ceiling coverings. For example, one builder may wish to lay the particle board before any wall-surface materials such as gypsum board or paneling are installed. The rationale may be that there will be less chance of damage to wall surfaces and ceilings from rough handling of the large, heavy boards. Another builder may opt for this risk to avoid the mess to the top surface of the particle board, such as gobs of dropped drywall compound, spilled stain, gouges from dropped tools, and other residuals of the finishing process. A third builder may compromise by putting down the particle board in all places except those where linoleum or tile will be laid with adhesive binders, places like an entryway, bathroom, utility room, and kitchen. Adhesives require a clean surface for adequate binding to take place.

Special area underlayment is determined by the uses that are served. All or most of the areas mentioned in the foregoing paragraph are to some extent subjected to moisture. Particle board is not recommended for underlayment where it may be subjected to liquid saturation at anytime. If there is any doubt of this statement, one can perform a simple test. Place a small strip of particle board half immersed in a container of water overnight. Take it out the next day, measure the thickness of the wet end, and compare it to the thickness of the dry end. The swelling that results will not go back to the original thickness after it dries. In time, repeated soakings will usually cause the particles of wood to separate from their glue bond. The board reverts back to a crumbled mass of loose chips. In fairness to the manufacturing industry, it should be noted that more durable products are constantly being developed. Waferboard, for example, is made of larger chips of wood bonded with waterproof glue. It does not disintegrate with repeated soakings.

Waterproof underlayment is needed in the bathroom, kitchen, and laundry. It is so easy to ignore this and simply floor the entire house with a common nonwaterproof board that it happens repeatedly. The unfortunate result is experienced at a later date when a water closet (toilet) has to be reset and the floor around it replaced. Sometimes the condition has progressed to an advanced stage of rotting so that floor joists and other structural parts are affected. Dry rot (a fungus condition) is often accelerated by the presence of dampness, humidity, and occasional wetting from plumbing leaks and dripping condensation.

Before purchasing the underlayment for damp areas, give some thought to the *transition junction*, where one type of flooring meets another. An objective is to keep the finished levels as nearly the same as possible. This can frequently be arranged by using a different-thickness board in the specialty area. The common board thickness for most of the house will probably be ⅝″ (particle board). A bathroom with inlaid linoleum adjacent to a wall-to-wall carpeted corridor will benefit from a ¾″ waterproof-grade plywood. The added thickness plus linoleum will more nearly equalize the levels at the junction. Another feasible combination is to use a second layer of exterior-grade ¼″ plywood over a common-height layer of exterior-grade plywood. Remember that the best system of tub installation is to have the underlayment and linoleum both run under the tub, so it must be installed before the frame walls are covered. The flooring must be zealously protected from that moment on.

Use adhesive in addition to ringed nails or screws to secure ¼″ ply underlayment to other underlayment. Cut and dry fit all the required pieces first. Then take up and remove the pieces and set them aside. Run parallel beads of adhesive 4″ apart across a workable area to form a grid pattern. Work rapidly. Replace the fitted boards in position. Quarter-inch plywood is fairly flexible and demands the best possible nailing routine to prevent crowning (rising up between nails). Use ring shank nails every 8″ along the joists and every 4″ along the edges of the plywood. Place a nail every 8″ between the joists. Stagger these to center between the nails that are in the joists. The result will be a flat, solid base that will last for decades.

Junction strips to cover the transition line between two different floor coverings are obtainable in a variety of materials, such as chromed steel, aluminum, wood, or vinyl. The strip bridges any difference in levels. It holds down the edges of materials and prevents scuffing. The strip provides a low profile ramp to help prevent tripping.

Countertops are another area vulnerable to moisture deterioration. Although many factories use particle board for the core material for preformed countertops, it is not recommended for home-built cabinets. Edges and corners chip off easily. Screws strip out easily. Most important, it is not waterproof. A leaky faucet may seem like a minor irritation. When it leads to a major repair job due to a disintegrated countertop, the significance of waterproof wood will be fully understood.

VAPOR BARRIER UNDERLAYMENT

A vapor barrier of 15-pound weight building paper is customarily installed between floor sheathing and particle board underlay or strip wood flooring. This asphalt-saturated paper is sometimes called felt. A roll contains 450 square feet. With a minimum lap, the roll will cover about 400 square feet.

The floor must be very clean and free of all bumps or obtrusions above the sheathing. Check for nailheads and gobs of drywall compound. Protruding nails are easy to spot, as they are worn shiny from traffic. Occasionally, a sheet of plywood has had an extra scrap of ply pressed into its surface at the factory. If it protrudes, it should be removed. Pull it off with the claws of your hammer or plane, or power sand it down to the surface level. Sweep away all debris. Vacuum to remove any particles overlooked.

Lay the building paper adjacent to the longest exterior wall first. The joint along the exterior sole plate and the subfloor should be caulked before fastening this sheet to ensure against infiltration. Allow ½″ of the paper to fold up over the caulked joint (Fig. 2-68). The combination of caulk and paper will prevent any potential infiltration of air under the sole. The surface of the paper prevents infiltration of air or moisture from beneath the floor.

Lap the next piece of paper over to the first white line on the black felt, approximately 2″. Put only a few staples in to hold the paper. One every 4′ is plenty. Remove any staples later that cause rippling of the paper as the underlayment or flooring boards are laid.

The building paper vapor barrier is omitted only when underlayment flooring, plywood or particle board, is glued to the subfloor (the U.S. Plywood recommended system). The paper serves several purposes in addition to forming a vapor and infiltration barrier. It aids in sound control between stories. It

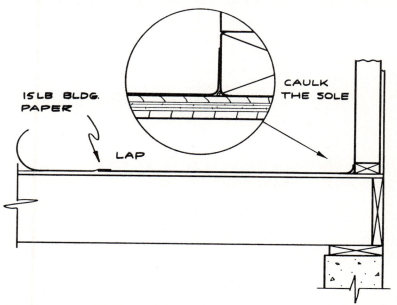

Figure 2-68 Caulking around the exterior sole plate and turned up building paper provide a good infiltration seal at the edges and throughout the floor.

forms a cushion over uneven surfaces. It deadens squeaks. Its greasy surface aids in driving strip tongue-and-groove boards tightly together.

11 WOOD FLOORS

Although wall-to-wall carpet currently accounts for the greatest square footage of flooring, there will continue to be calls for tongue-and-groove strip flooring and parquet flooring. *Parquet* (pronounced par-kay) means "small square." A finished wood floor is laid before the installation of baseboard and base shoe.

WOOD PARQUET FLOORING

Wood parquet (Fig 2-69) is usually fabricated from thin narrow T&G (tongue-and-groove) strips of hardwood. The strips are glued together to form a square. Then the edges are tongued on two adja-

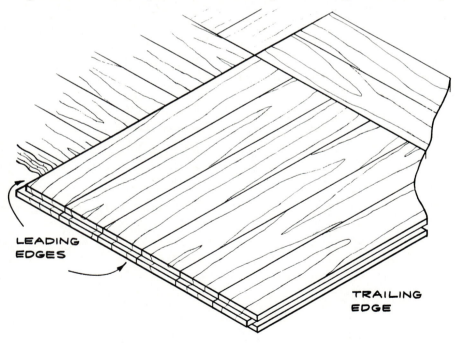

Figure 2-69 Parquet flooring is prefabricated in squares that are laid progressively with the tongued edges leading. The bonding agent is adhesive.

cent sides and grooved on the others. When assembled on the underlayment (required in addition to sheathing), a checkerboard pattern results from the alternating strip grain. Although expensive, the parquet floor is popular for entryways and other special nooks. Wood parquet is installed with adhesive much like square tile. If a piece is warped and offers resistance to lying flat, a small brad may be driven at an angle through the leading tongue. It is always advisable to predrill a hole to prevent the thin hardwood from splitting.

The pattern of layment is either to have a seam or a full tile at the center lines of the room. This most frequently results in cut pieces around the perimeter (partial tiles). The cut-off pieces will frequently be usable as starters and finishers in every other course. This will be the case where the dimensions of the room accommodate so many tile units plus a little less than half of one more unit on each side.

Most parquet flooring comes prefinished. The floor is complete after it is laid. It should be rolled or walked on immediately to assure contact and spreading of the adhesive. When comparing costs of finished floor types, remember to add the cost of proper underlayment panels for those types that are glued.

STRIP FLOORING

T&G strip flooring is available in both hard and soft wood. The traditional hardwoods most commonly used are oak and maple. The softwoods used are fir and pine. In cities where a half-dozen or more lumberyards exist, there is usually one that specializes in vintage materials. If you have use for a newel post, some five-quarter pine, or a wooden closet rung, the company that has these items will likely carry tongue-and-groove flooring.

Characteristics of T&G hardwood are unique. For example, it comes in bundles of various length ranges. "Shorts" are bundles of 12 to 18″ in length or 12″ to 24″, or whatever the mill designates. The longer the bundle range, the higher the price. Long lengths bring a premium price, but these pieces are laid faster and make a stiffer floor.

The T&G flooring board is said to be *end matched*. This means that one end has a tongue while the other has a groove. These tongues and grooves dictate the direction taken while laying the floor. The first board is laid with the edge groove toward the wall that is perpendicular to the floor joists. This is a hard-and-fast rule that must never be violated when ½″ sheathing is used. Running parallel to the joists will cause ripples, sags, and a squeaky floor. The tongued end is positioned next to the adjacent wall (Fig. 2-70). From there on the tongued edge and tongued end will be in the leading exposed position. The piece that reaches the other wall is cut a little short (up to about ¼″). This amount of space is left all around the room between the flooring and the walls for expansion. The first piece will have to be blocked out to keep it from driving against the wall. The spacer blocks may be removed after several boards are nailed. The cut-off end of the last board in each course is taken to the opposite side of the room to start the next course, since it does not require the grooved end adjacent to the wall.

Nailing is a particular job. The first strip requires surface nailing on the edge adjacent to the wall. *Drill tap holes* slightly smaller than the nail shank diameter. Each tap hole must be centered over a joist. The hole should be as close to the edge of the board as possible without entering the groove (about ½″ from the edge). The baseboard and base shoe will then cover the nailhead.

Nails on the lead edge are started in the corner formed by the top of the tongue. The angle is about 50 to 60°. Some flooring can be nailed without pretapping a hole. If it is noted that a crack devel-

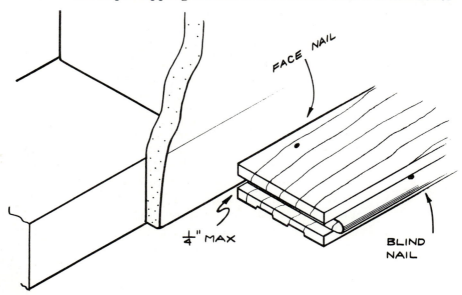

Figure 2-70 The first piece of flooring leads with the tongue and is surface nailed under the baseboard and shoe.

ops on each side of the nail, then tap holes should be drilled routinely.

Nails have evolved from the rectangular cut nail familiar to retrofitters through the cut-head finish nail to the screw-shanked, tempered wedge head. The latter will rarely bend and is stiff enough to pass through hardwood with little deflection.

Sinking the head calls for a unique technique. Cup-head finishing nails are sunk flush with the tapered cupped point of a nailset. The tempered flooring nail causes the nailset to bounce off the head and damage the tongue. The Stanley nail set and any other square-headed set is adapted for setting the wedge-head tempered nail. The nail is driven to a point where it can no longer be hit without damaging the wood (Fig. 2-71). The nailset is then laid with the square head flat in the trough on top of the tongue.

Place the round shank of the nailset over the nail. Position it with the nail under the full diameter of the shank just above the tapered end. Rap the set smartly over this point while holding it in place. The nailhead will be sunk flush enough to clear the groove of the next board.

Driving the boards tightly together is accomplished by using a short length of the same T&G board. Match the groove

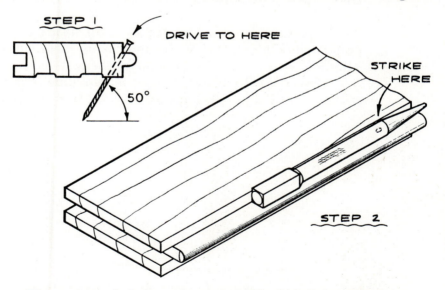

Figure 2-71   Sink the nail with the side of a nail set to avoid damage to the wood from hammer marks or from splitting of the tongue of the board with the point of the nail set if it should slip off the hardened flooring nail.

over the tongue of the board being driven. With your hammer head lying flat on its side on the floor, rap the tongue side of the block. Also use this block on the end of the new board to drive it onto the end tongue of the preceding board; then work the long edge into place. Drive and set the nails. Sometimes the nails will not pull the board up tightly. Use the block again and reset the nails. It is easy to get T&G boards out of parallel by forcing them tighter together at the ends or in the middle. After four or five courses are laid, check the parallelism by measuring from three or four places along the lead edge back to the starting wall.

The last board usually has to be ripped, as the distance remaining is less than the board width. Also, the space may not be parallel with the wall. Custom rip the board to the same dimension that exists from the wall to the *edge* of the tongue on the previous board laid. This will permit the final piece to be dropped in and wedged onto the tongue with a wonder bar or ripping bar (Fig. 2-72). It is drilled for surface nails the same as the first board. Keep pressure on the bar to hold the joint closed while sinking each nail. Again, it is very important to anchor each nail in a joist.

UNFINISHED FLOORING

Sanding is required of unfinished strip flooring. Floor finishers prefer not to have door jambs and casing installed at the time of sanding, as it is so easy to damage them.

Closed-grain wood such as maple, pine, and fir require no grain filler. They will, however, benefit from a deep penetrating

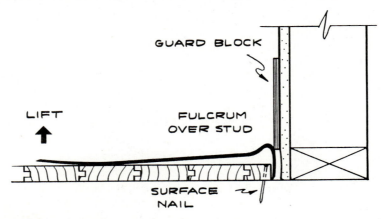

Figure 2-72 Either end of a wonder bar provides leverage to squeeze on the last board and hold it tightly while each nail is driven.

sealer. Oak is open grained, which means that there are long cavities running with the grain figure. To obtain a smooth surface that is easier to clean, a paste filler is rubbed into the open grain. The excess is rubbed off flush with the surface. Burlap works well to remove the excess. Coarse shavings will also work, but the polluted shavings must be constantly brushed away from the working area to assure that the grain is adequately filled and the excess filler is all removed. Liquid fillers are available and are moderately successful. The problem with any liquid of heavy viscosity is that it tends to bridge a grain opening, thereby forming an air pocket underneath. As the liquid dries, it shrinks. The bridge breaks and the gap is exposed again much as it was before. Regardless of which filler type is used, a thorough, close-range inspection should be made before proceeding with the finishing coats. Unfilled spots or areas will show up as a slightly different color when the finish is put on.

Door jambs and casings will be fitted snugly on top of the finished floor surface.

□ PARTICLE BOARD UNDERLAYMENT

There are three systems of installing the second layer of floor for carpet underlayment. Strangely, the variance in method is dictated partially by the type of roof framing that exists. For example, a house with a trussed roof that does not depend on interior bearing partitions for support may be wisely erected as a shell initially, for any of three reasons. First, it will be closed in against the weather sooner. Second, the entire interior can be floored as a single unit (Fig. 2-73), thus avoiding much labor time. Third, the floor will be considerably stiffer under and around partitions.

A modification of the unified technique is to raise only the center or centrally located bearing partitions upon which the ceiling joists of a stick-built roof depend for support (Fig. 2-74). With this variance, large near-halves of the house may be floored without the interruption of many little partitions. The time taken to floor half the house will be little, if any, more than it will take to floor a single bedroom with his-and-her closets and a bathroom attached.

The third method is the traditional way of erecting all partitions on the subfloor initially. The particle board then requires much measuring, cutting, and seemingly endless fitting throughout the maze of partitions.

Figure 2-73 Floor underlayment installation is greatly simplified by the open building system.

Figure 2-74 A single, centrally located bearing wall (partially studded) permits a major part of the underlayment to be installed with few obstructions.

FULL-FLOOR LAYMENT

Full-floor layment in conjunction with the open interior building concept has so many good things going for it that it is highly recommended by the author. Remember the special techniques for bracing throughout the sequence, as therein lies the safety of the technique.

All particle board *ends* should terminate at and over the center of a joist. Begin by rolling out two courses of building paper perpendicularly to the floor joists and parallel to the long exterior walls. In this manner the joists can be located at the wall junction directly under a stud, provided that the direct in-line modular system of framing has been followed. Two courses of paper will cover a width of a little less than 6'. Therefore, the floor sheathing will be exposed from there on, which exposes the end joints and field nails in the sheathing. If these are properly placed, the joists will be locatable by reference. A line between the field reference and stud reference *should* locate the joist accurately. Where there is doubt, a final technique is to drive a nail through the sheathing ¾" right or left of the expected joist center; then go under the house and locate it. If the nail hits solid wood, move farther away from the assumed center line ¼" at a time. There will be an entirely different feeling when the nail misses the joist. It is extremely important to place the first sheet properly, as all those to follow depend on it. Remember that the joists are accurately centered on 16", but that some of the sheathing sheets have been shortened to provide expansion gaps.

Starting the first sheet requires custom cutting to length. The length will be a half- or full-sheet module minus the exterior wall depth and a small clearance gap between the sole and the underlayment. The author has for many years practiced a technique related to this gap that eliminates a future problem. With precut studs, a ½" drywall ceiling, and a ⅝" thick particle board underlayment, the remaining height in the room is exactly 96". Since rough framing is never perfect, it becomes impossible to sandwich two 4' horizontal courses of drywall or an 8'-high sheet of paneling into this theoretical space. Therefore, much cutting is involved to fit the lower course. To avoid this problem completely, the particle board underlay is spaced out away from the wall sole about ½ to ⅝". This allows a ⅝" clearance adapter, which is identical to that existing with slab floors. It also provides room for a floor raiser to be slipped under the edge of the board or panel.

The lead edge of the underlayment should be the uncut factory end. It is likely to be perfectly square and straight. Place the on-site cut end adjacent to the sole. Strike a chalk line the full length of the black paper. This line will be 4'⅝" away from each corner at the ends of the run. Do not align the particle board sheets with the wall. Align them with the chalk line.

Lay two sheets along the first course. No more! Put only four temporary nails in each of these. Leave the nails exposed so that they can be pulled. Unlike intentionally separated sheathing, the underlayment should be as tightly joined as possible. Start a third roll of paper. Unroll it far enough to assure a proper lap. Staple part of it with as few staples as possible. Start a second course of underlayment. The lead piece of the second course will be of such a length as to set up a 50 percent staggering pattern (Fig. 2-75). Align this sheet and tack temporarily. Now lay the second sheet of the second course. At this point the potential exists for tightly joining all edges and ends of the four pieces, in perfect alignment with the stringline. Loosen the nails and gently tap them into alignment as required until all joints are tight and headed straight down the chalk line.

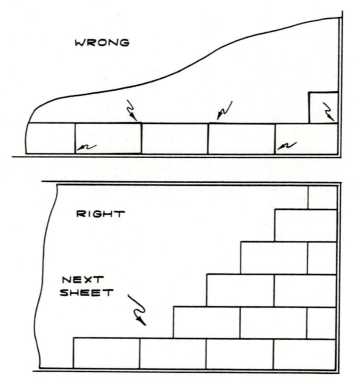

Figure 2-75 Each board helps align those alongside when laid as seen in the "right" pattern shown in the lower view. Laid as shown in the upper view, even to a chalk line, small discrepancies at the end joints will compound into sizable cracks along the edges.

Laying the rest of the particle board throughout the open space continues in the same manner. Never let a course run more than one sheet ahead of another. Keep all courses progressing at once in a staggered pattern. Never nail down a sheet permanently that is running out ahead with no sheets alongside to guarantee the integrity of the whole. By following this technique, an entire floor of a house can be laid so well that the edge of a piece of paper cannot be slipped into any joint between the underlay sheets. The pride in such workmanship is a far more permanent reward than any that money can buy.

Major modular floor widths such as 24' (six sheets across) and 28' (seven sheets across) will net an edge lap over the sheathing joint equal to the wall depth and inset amount of the particle board. This is about 4" with a 2 × 4 wall. The mid mod house depth of 26' width or wings of 14, 18, or 22' will have half-width sheets of sheathing on one side or the other. A larger lapover is achieved by starting the underlayment on the side of the house where the half-sheets of sheathing are. By so doing, the lap will be much closer to the center of the sheathing panels and consequently offer the potential for a stiffer floor. The same theory and practice hold true when considering where to start in terms of end lapping. End joints of the underlayment should *never* be allowed to match those of the sheathing. Such an arrangement would create a significant absence of stiffness in a localized area. The best setup is to have all joints in the two layers staggered apart from each other as far as possible. If the subfloor sheathing starts with a full sheet, start the first particle board with a sub-half-piece, or vice versa. From there on, all joints will automatically be lapped correctly.

HALF-FLOOR LAYMENT

The next best alternative is to lay the floor in halves completely. This potential presents itself where only a center bearing partition is in place at this point of development. This is a very feasible technique. It approaches the full-open concept in benefits and falls short only in two areas. It eliminates the good effects of a full tie over the center line of the house. This is not a serious loss, however, as particle board does not contain a lot of tensile strength as does plywood. Where plywood sheathing has been arranged to run over the center junction of the floor joist, the need for the particle board to do the same is minimal. The other objectionable feature from the intrusion of the partition is the extra labor time needed to cut and fit two more joints, one on each side of the long wall.

TRADITIONAL LAYMENT

Laying particle board in the traditionally framed house is at best a time-consuming nuisance once a person has experienced the rapidity and "clean" joinery of the open-layment method. Where *all* the partitions are in place at the outset of the underlayment task, the job will still employ all the placement rules described earlier. The difference is that every room is a separate entity, an island unto itself, with which to deal. No master plan evolves. All the turns and door jamb jutouts must be measured, laid out on the board, and cut. Many butt joints will be saw cut on the job. Little continuity of factory edges will exist except in the central areas of large rooms. This involves much more linear area for error and careful fitting. It is not a difficult job for a competent craftsman with high-quality goals, but it does present a challenge that is avoidable by accepting the validity and many benefits of either of the open-concept techniques.

BRACING

Bracing is so important as to warrant special attention. Since there are no braced partitions to strengthen the exterior walls in the open concept, a diagonal brace to the floor every 8' to 10' is called for down the wall while construction is underway. As soon as the laying of particle board is begun, these braces are removed *one at a time* and reset immediately from the bottom of a stud up to a ceiling joist. By so doing, the floor area is cleared so that the papering and boarding can proceed uninhibited.

NAILING

Nailing particle board is unique to other forms of wood. Particle board has some characteristics that require consideration. The board is comprised of such small particles of wood that it has no grain direction in the cellular sense. This might be considered an asset when compared to true wood, but it is not. The particle board simply crumbles and whole chunks break away as compared to wood, which cracks and splinters but does not disintegrate. Because there are no large cells but only small chips surrounded by adhesive, there is no place for a nail to expand its surrounding. How does this affect nailing? Unfortunately, it affects it in several negative ways. Nails in the field will break out a crater on the back side, unless firm contact with the anchoring surface is maintained. This makes it extremely important to nail only over and into floor joists. A nail driven in unbacked sheathing will bounce the sheathing away from the particle board with each blow. A crater usually breaks ahead of the nail point before the nail penetrates the flexible wood intended to anchor it. The chips that push out comprise a lump between the surfaces, which in turn causes a slight hump. When hit again, the head of the nail fractures its way through above the crater and all holding power is lost.

Edges are equally vulnerable in different ways. The wood close to an edge easily breaks away when a nail is pounded excessively in an attempt to sink the head below the surface. Corners are especially vulnerable to breakage. A major cause of edge breaking is the use of nails of too large diameter. The hardened flooring nail is an excellent choice for particle board. Its sectional shape displaces a path easier and its holding power is superior. Coated nails are also a good choice. Their diameter is smaller than that of a common nail. The heads are thinner and gently countersunk for easier entry. Common nails are a poor choice for all the opposite reasons. In some instances, drilling tap holes will be the only way to avoid damage from nails. The practice is recommended for difficult end-nailing situations.

Nail spacing on particle board follows the same objectives as any type of sheet decking. About one and one-half times as many are placed on the ends as are placed across the field. With shorter nails and joists of power-holding characteristics (softer), more nails or longer nails for greater penetration will be needed. Generally, the range for distribution will be 8″ in the field with 6″ on the ends to 6″ in the field with 4″ on the ends. Do not nail the particle board between the joists into ½″ sheathing. It is too thin and springy to hold adequately. If the building paper shows a tendency to bulge up in front or under the particle board, pull the staples ahead and let the board press the paper down as you go.

Permanent nailing may progress on any sheet that is surrounded by lead sheets. Only after there remains no doubt that a sheet will not be moved should all the nails be installed permanently. It is almost impossible to take up a sheet of particle board without destroying it after nails have been driven home in several places.

An advantage of grain-free particle board is found where working on small, confined floor places. Unlike plywood, which must cross the joists at right angles with the major number of plies, particle board may be laid in any direction. Its strength is equal both crosswise and lengthwise of a sheet.

Remember that, where the particle board has been applied to a half or whole floor without interfering partitions, all those partitions to be built will require studs reduced in length by an amount equal to the thickness of the underlayment material.

12 INTEGRATED DOOR JAMB SYSTEM

An integrated system for interior door framing and casing is ready-made for the carpenter who recognizes the simplicity and benefits. It begins by framing the rough opening with a single 2 × 10 header centered in the depth of the wall with a flat 2 × 4 under the header, which bears on the vertical trimmers to complete the common vertical plane of the rough opening (Fig. 2-76).

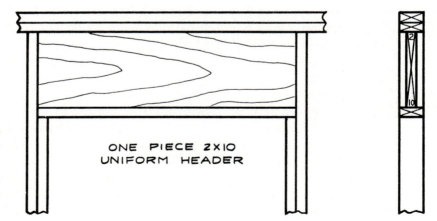

ONE PIECE 2×10
UNIFORM HEADER

Figure 2-76 The single 2 × 10 with a lower plate trimmer has many advantages during and after construction.

The door jambs are butted up under this style of header (Fig. 2-77). The bottoms of the side jambs will *not* rest on the floor, but will be up about ⅜ to ½″ above the carpet-underlayment particle board. Wall-to-wall carpet installers appreciate this gap, as it permits pad and carpeting to run under the jamb. It avoids the down-slanted surface (tacked through the doorway), which holds dust and dirt. Of course, jambs adjacent to tile flooring should be set exactly to clear the thickness of linoleum, vinyl, or ceramic tile (Fig. 2-78). Some contractors prefer to lay these floor coverings before the jambs are set, which eliminates precision cutting around the jambs and stops and permits the jambs to be set directly on the

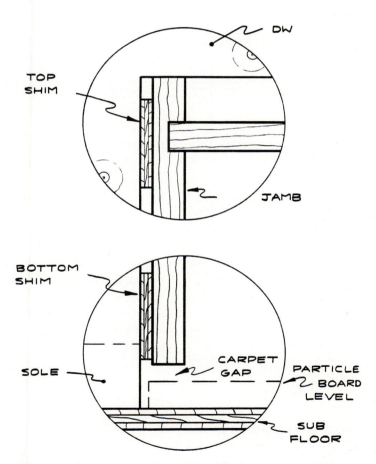

Figure 2-77 The single 2 × 10 uniform header with a flat 2 × 4 makes it possible to hang a precut door jamb without alteration where wall-to-wall carpet is specified.

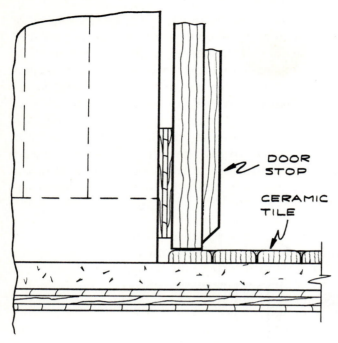

DOOR STOP

CERAMIC TILE

Figure 2-78 Jambs over linoleum or other hard floor coverings should be custom fitted to rest on top the surface. If the jamb is hung first, leave the proper space so the tile can be run under the jamb.

finished surface. Where jambs rest on the floor, the stop should be mitered upward at a 45° angle to eliminate interference with carpet and linoleum.

A door hung in the uniform-headed opening will swing about 1″ above the finished floor. This is ideal to accommodate both the rug-clearance and cold-air-return objectives.

Many books still quote the old 82″ rough-in height as a standard. It is no longer high enough. Those who choose to use a built-up 4 × 4 or 4 × 6 header with cripple studs (in spite of the advantages of the single unit header) should make the rough opening height 83 to 83½″ high for all locations where carpeting will be used. Failure to do so will result in the necessity of sawing off a portion of the door (a poor and unnecessary practice).

JAMB KIT

Jambs can be made from stock lumber. It is seldom cost effective to fabricate a jamb set this way, however, unless an economical source of clear lumber is available and one has a table saw and a jointer and lots of unpaid time.

An interior jamb kit consists of two side jambs and a head jamb. All these pieces are slightly beveled on the edges (3 to 5°). The wide side of each beveled board faces toward the opening. It is not possible to assemble the sides incorrectly because there is a dado (a crossgrain groove) at the top of each side jamb into which the headboard fits. It *is* possible to assemble the headboard upside down. The wide side of the bevel-edged headboard faces down.

Cutting the headboard to length takes some thought and care if one is to avoid the necessity of door planing later. The total length of the headboard will be the sum of the actual door width plus the sum of the depths of the two dados plus the sum of the two clearance gaps at the hinge and latch side of the door. The latter figure is the only variable in the summation.

There are two schools of thought about door clearance. One school says to make the clearance wide and ample enough so that there is no possibility of binding, chafing, or sticking should the door swell in humid times of year. The other school champions a perfect ⅛″ uniform crack all around the top and sides.

Flush-morticed hinges will dictate the clearance to be that of the gap between the hinge leaves when held parallel in the closed position. It will be ⅛″. There is no rationale for varying this clearance on the hinge side, as door swelling will show up only on the latch side.

To successfully open and close a door with ⅛″ clearance on the latch-side position, it is advisable to bevel the latch edge. A square edge will not have adequate clearance. The installer must bear in mind that two or three coats of varnish or paint will add enough thickness to close the intended gap.

Advocates of a larger latch-side clearance, such as ³⁄₁₆ to ¼″, will cite the advantages of nonbeveling, plus the fact that the latch bolt faceplate is morticed flush to the square edge and looks neater than one seemingly canted across a beveled edge (Fig. 2-79). Geographical areas of great seasonal variance in temperature and/or humidity will find the wide clearance to be less troublesome.

Prehung doors are sometimes fitted too tightly and will require planing. The prehung door that has been bored for a lockset and fits too tightly will require square planing on the hinge edge only since the hole for the door knob cannot be altered. The hinges will require remorticing. The amount required to be planed off may be as much or more than the depth of the original mortices. Maintain the indexing (the exact location) of each hinge by deep-

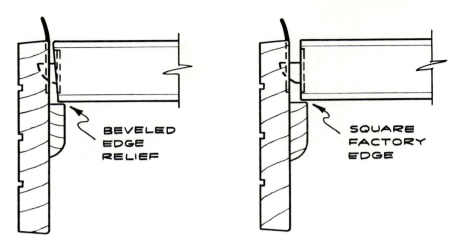

Figure 2-79 Two alternative techniques of fitting a door relate to the length that the head board jamb must be cut.

ening the perimeter of the mortice with a chisel before planing. Then plane off the necessary relief and remortice the hinge butt. The chisel marks will indicate the exact location of the new mortices.

JAMB DEPTH

Two standardized jamb depth sizes are available from the lumberyard. The smaller of the two accommodates the drywall system. It is 4½″ deep to span a 3½″ stud with a ½″ layer of gypsum wallboard on each side. This jamb size will also fit a ¼″ paneled partition with an underlayment backing of ¼″ gypsum board (¼″-thick gypsum is not stocked universally).

Jambs for wet-plaster jobs may be difficult to find because their primary use is in retrofit remodeling. In larger cities there is usually at least one lumberyard that specializes in vintage items. With some tools or power equipment, any jamb that is large enough to begin with can be machined to a custom fit.

INSTALLING A PREHUNG DOOR

A prehung door usually includes the surrounding jambs assembled and sometimes cased and a door with hinges morticed and attached to the jamb. The jambs have door stops attached to all three sides. No lockset is furnished, although the door may be bored to receive one. The assembled kit is available in right- or left-hand-swinging formation.

Installing the prehung door kit is simple and quick. Leave the door in the jamb. Set the whole assembly in the opening. Block it up off the floor to the desired height. Occasionally, the header is not perfectly level. In such a case, block the jamb tightly up under the *low* side of the header. Block up the other side only high enough to maintain a parallel clearance between the door top and the head jamb after the hinged jamb has been plumbed.

Most kits have two temporary nails driven through the jamb into the door at the bottom and top of the latch side to keep the jamb from breaking away while being handled. These nails must be removed before inserting the kit all the way into the opening. Wait until the last moment to remove these nails. Block the jambs immediately after pulling the nails. This is important because, once pulled, the weight of the door can drop the hinge side only and crack open all the corner joints in the casing or jamb dados. Some kits do not include casing.

Most kits have cardboard or plastic spacer shims stapled or taped between the door and jamb on the latch side and top. These spacers maintain the proper clearance during installation. Take them off and discard them after the door set is firmly nailed in place.

Shim the jambs at the critical locations: top and bottom, behind the hinges, and behind the striker plates. The prehung jamb and door should not be suspended only from the casing, which is nailed to the wall. The kit may have one side of the jambs pretrimmed, and packaged trim is furnished for the other side. In this case, shim the jambs from the open side, being careful not to drive the casing off the other side. Kits without prefitted casing are simply custom cased after installation. Some builders prefer to do this after wall painting is completed.

At one time, jamb thickness was as much as ⅞″. In a rough opening 2″ wider than the door, there was very little space left for shimming if the door was left full width (few were). Now the prefabricated jambs of some brands are milled to a scant ⅝″ thickness. Some economy types are fabricated from short lengths of wood that are *finger joined* and glued. This jamb will have more than ample shimming space in a rough opening 2″ more than the door width. In fact, one may wish to precut and make use of plywood shims of

3 mm, ¼″, ⅜″, and ½″ scrap to take up the excess space. These 2″ ×
3″ blocks may be nailed to the trimmer studs at the correct locations before plumbing and leveling of the jambs. Tapered shim
shingles are positioned on a block spacer or used alone for infinite
adjustment (Fig. 2-80). There should always be a wide block about
3″ × 4″ behind each hinge where a gap exists so that long replacement screws will not have to jump across to reach the trimmer
stud. Unless the door is to be centered in an opening or corridor, it
is best to place the jamb against the trimmer on the hinge side and
space it out only enough to make it plumb and straight.

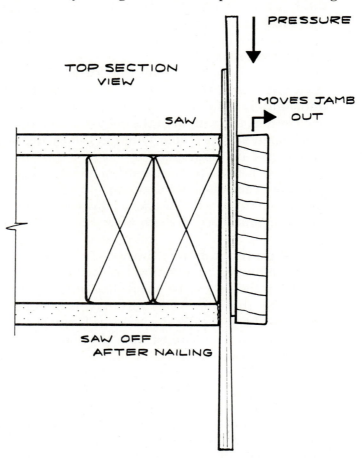

Figure 2-80 Typical shingle shimming of a fairly wide gap to produce a straight and plumb door jamb. Excessively wide gaps may be
shimmed with a block of the exact size needed or a combination of
shingles on a block.

Nailing of the jamb may proceed as soon as the assembly is firmed in place with temporary floor blocks and permanent shims. Where there is need to hide the mounting nails, the door stop is removed from the jambs. Do this very carefully using a stiff putty knife or a wide wood chisel to ease under an edge and gently pry away the stop (Fig. 2-81). Place each nail in the jamb only where the stop, when replaced, will cover the nail. Use nails with heads (finish nails with little cup heads have inferior drawdown ability). Number 6 or 7d box nails will hold well. Sink all heads flush with the surface. Nail only through the shims (a plywood shim is superior because it will not split).

Test the door swing. Remove the factory spacers and work the door through its intended arc. There should be no strain on the

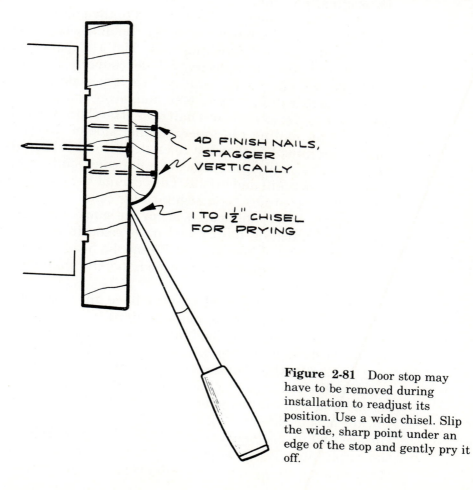

4D FINISH NAILS, STAGGER VERTICALLY

1 TO 1½" CHISEL FOR PRYING

Figure 2-81 Door stop may have to be removed during installation to readjust its position. Use a wide chisel. Slip the wide, sharp point under an edge of the stop and gently pry it off.

hinges in any position, no bind, and no reluctance to close fully. Make adjustments in the jamb where the door clearance is considered excessive, undersize, or unparallel so that the clearance will be adequate after finishing materials have been added.

A typical binding area is the door stop contact on the hinge side. About a $1/16''$ clearance is needed there between the door face and the edge of the stop. A factory "prehung" may come through with no clearance there. At the assembly plant, the door is put in the jamb, and the stops are butted to the door and stapled or power nailed to the jamb. After varnishing or painting, the junction is too tight. Set the stop back from the door when reinstalling it. This will necessitate using new nails first in different locations so that the originals do not fall into the old holes and pull the stop back to its original position.

Nail the casing onto the wall and to the jamb to complete the job. There is an alternative to the poor holding characteristic of the traditional cup-head finishing nail. The $1\frac{1}{2}''$ panel nail on the outer thicker side of the casing will do a superb job of drawing the casing down tightly to the wall surface. It seldom splits the casing, as the sharp annular rings tear and sever the grain instead of wedging it apart as a smooth nail does. The shorter panel nails are excellent for nailing the inner, thinner side of the casing to the jamb. Care must be taken not to angle the nail to the surface. The head must be flat to the surface if a puttying job is to be avoided. Panel nails are stiff and brittle. They cannot be bent to square up a head with the surface as a regular nail can.

The head of a panel nail is about the same diameter as that of a cup-head finishing nail. Panel nails come in enough colors to meet most needs. Where possible to set the head square and flush to the surface, no putty will be needed, thereby eliminating a time-consuming detail.

Some factory-installed casings have the top corner miters locked in alignment with metal splines. Corners that are not splined can be effectively held in alignment by driving a $1\frac{1}{2}''$ panel nail down through the top casing into the end grain of the side casing (Fig. 2-82), while holding the face of the casing in perfect alignment. A little carpenter glue on the surface of each miter before assembling will aid the joint's permanency. Place the nail in the thicker part of the molding about $1/2''$ in from the corner. The first surface nail on each side of the corner should be kept away from the corner about $4''$ so as not to pressure or crack the miter joint open. Apply these two nails simultaneously with alternating ham-

RINGED PANEL NAIL

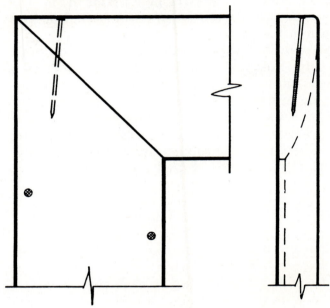

Figure 2-82   Long ringed panel nails are excellent corner miter fasteners.

mer blows. The final seating is done with a nailset and very gentle taps of a finish-weight hammer (13 oz. or less).

The latch hardware ("doorknob") of a nonlocking type is called a *passage set*. A set that locks from one side only is called a *privacy set* (used on bathroom doors). The type used on exterior entrances is referred to as a *keyed entrance set*. *Common keyed* means that security-type locks can be purchased in groups of two or more locks that use the same key. All types include an instruction sheet for proper installation.

13   CABINET INSTALLATION

It is a rarity for cabinets to be built on site nowadays as they frequently were during the painted-cabinet period from the 1930s through the 1950s. Ready-made finished cabinets in many styles are available from most cashway lumber dealers, as well as other building supply centers. Some savings may be realized by constructing all parts of kitchen and bath cabinetry on site except the face frames, doors, and drawer fronts. These parts may be ordered from a custom cabinet shop to face site-built frames and shelves.

Constructing finished cabinetry is not a job for the novice. It is a skilled trade requiring an extensive investment in machines and equipment and much experience.

Hanging preassembled top cabinets requires minimum tools and a little help. Purchased cabinets usually have lightweight plywood backs, often as thin as 3 mm (about ⅛"). No attempt should be made to use this type of back for attaching the cabinet to the wall. Screws should pass through only solid wood frame members into the wall studs. These horizontal frames are found at the top and bottom of the cabinet and sometimes under shelves. They are usually about 1½" high by ¾" deep.

LOCATING STUDS

Locating studs is done first by sound. Most cabinets will be located on a wall with at least one duplex electric outlet. The outlet is probably nailed to the side of a stud. Tap on each side of the box with your knuckle or hammer. The side that sounds and feels solid is where the stud is. Mark a point ¾" from the edge of the duplex box (not from a cover; Fig. 2-83). Hold a level vertically by the mark. Make another vertical mark at a point that will be just below the upper cabinet. Determine the area that will be covered by the cabinet. Make marks to right and left of the first pilot mark at each stud into which screws will be placed.

Probing through the wall board is the last-resort method of confirming the location of the structural anchors. Choose a spot that will be covered by the cabinet. Use the tapping and sound method to get close. Drive a small nail, number 4d or so, in the most likely spot. If it hits wood, pull it out and move right or left ¾" and puncture the wallboard again. Continue the practice until both edges of the stud are established. No more exploring should be required if all the other studs are spaced properly and are plumb. Measure from your pilot stud in multiples of 16" to right and left. Do not settle for a single exploratory nail that hits wood on the first try as an index. It could be very close to the edge of a stud. The center location is the goal for sure and sound anchorage. Magnetic "stud finders" do not find studs. They try to find drywall nailheads. Should a nail be off center (most are), the centering objective will be faulted as well.

INSTALLING UPPER CABINETS

Prepare some temporary braces to extend from the floor to the bottom of the cabinet. Each brace should be about ¼ to ½″ longer than the distance so that it can be wedged tightly in place, thus putting pressure on the underside of the cabinet ends. This will in turn press the top of the cabinet firmly up against the soffit. With a helper, hoist the cabinet into place and brace it to the floor. Locate and mark all places where supporting screws can be used, where screws will anchor in solid wood.

Use flat-head or oval-head screws. Round heads make future cleaning difficult. Drill screw holes at the center of the frame boards at each of the marked locations. The drill bit should be the same size as the screw shank or very slightly smaller. The shank of a screw is the smooth part between the head and the threads.

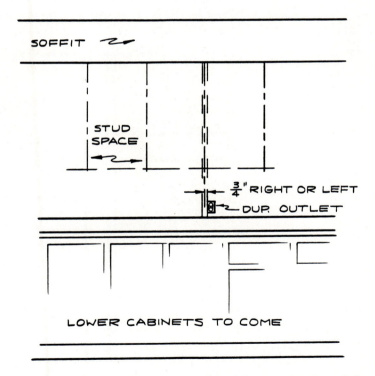

Figure 2-83 Locate studs behind a wall by referencing right or left of an electric box.

Countersink each hole so that the screw heads will be flush with the surface (Fig. 2-84).

Good-quality, shop-built cabinets have tops, bottoms, and shelves dadoed into solid ends. These are self-supporting on the face if supported adequately at the back. Screws in the top-mounting stringer will be tensile stressed in their effort to prevent the top of the cabinet from falling forward away from the wall. These top screws must be long in order to reach and hold in the studs (Fig. 2-85). These top screws may be placed horizontally, as the shear stress is placed primarily on the screws farther down below the lower shelves. Where front anchoring to the soffit is desired with this type of prefabricated cabinet, it may be achieved by carefully drilling pilot holes vertically through the front cabinet facing.

Module cabinets may be assembled with bolts or screws before raising or raised as individual units and then fastened together. Where the individual units to be gang assembled are small

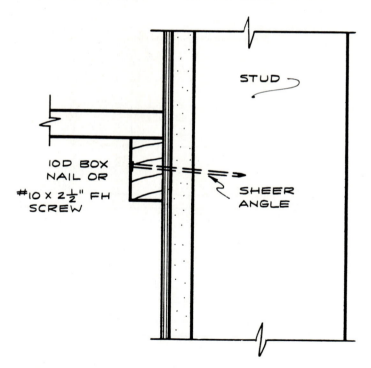

Figure 2-84 Shelf support rails provide a means of mounting top cabinets to the walls. Long, thin nails or screws with flat or oval heads may be used to fasten the cabinets to the studs.

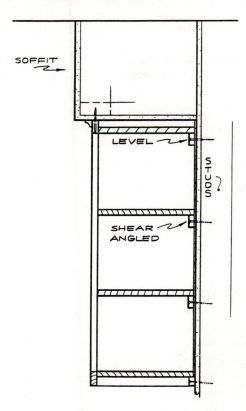

Figure 2-85 Factory- and
shop-made cabinet units usually
have dado-held shelves, thin
panel backs, and rails. Long
screws are needed to hold them to
the stud wall.

in width, it will be better to fasten several of them together before
hoisting them. Fasten as many units together as can handily be
put up. Some factory-made units come predrilled. Others are made
with face wood on both ends so that they can be used indepen-
dently or clustered. This type is usually undrilled. To gang-
assemble undrilled units, clamp them together first. Alignment
should be perfect. Start with a pair. Clamp them with C clamps or
handscrews, being careful not to damage any finished surfaces or
put unnecessary strain on any joints. Bar clamps are better for
small assemblies, but long bar clamps are seldom available outside
the cabinet shop.

INSTALLING FLOOR CABINETS

Installing floor cabinets is much simpler. They do not require temporary bracing or holding up. Base cabinets are simply put in
place, adjusted, leveled with shims, and attached to the wall studs

in a few solid places. Some preliminary work is usually required where wall fixtures exist.

Plumbing openings for supply pipes and drains must be located and drilled through cabinets that have backs or through bottoms where S traps are used instead of wall-routed P traps. Accuracy in locating and cutting these openings is important because the pipe flanges used to cover the gaps are only so big. Measurement is the least reliable way to transfer the pipe location to the cabinet back. Place the cabinet against the roughed-in plumbing stubs. Reach down behind the cabinet and outline the hole areas. Remember the dishwasher wiring and the garbage disposer hookup.

FINISHING

Joiner strips and corner adapters are stock items supplied to make the transition between cabinet units where they join and/or pass around corners. Cabinets do not always fit squarely into corners. Facing filler strips are obtainable to solve this problem. Your cabinet dealer will furnish specification sheets listing all these items, as well as the stock sizes of all the cabinets available.

Contoured countertops that meet at a perpendicular corner require mitering at a 45° angle in order for the rolled front lip and the splashback to match perfectly (Fig. 2-86). After dry fitting this joint to perfection, a backup board of ½ to ¾″ plywood should be glued and screwed to the underside to guarantee that the joint cannot separate. The board should be no less than 4″ wide so that a minimum of 2″ contacts each side of the joint. A larger piece will be beneficial in stiffening and leveling the corner joint. Be extremely careful not to permit any screw from seating so deeply that the point pushes up and/or cracks the laminate surface covering. Most preformed tops have the thinnest grade of laminate. Dry fit the entire assembly first; then disassemble it, apply the glue, and reassemble it in place.

The body of the preformed top is usually made of a dense particle board. Overpowered screws have a tendency to strip out. Just before applying the final turn, it may be prudent to back out the screw and rub a paraffin cube across the hole. The paraffin deposit will be pushed ahead of the screw into the seat. Draw the threads of the screw across the paraffin. Roll the screw threads be-

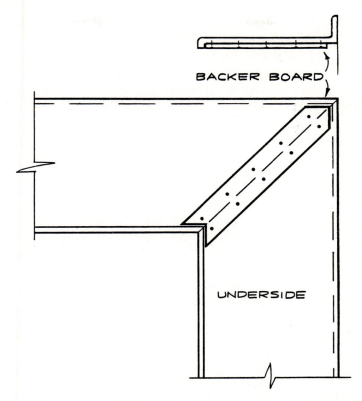

Figure 2-86 A preformed cabinet top that passes around a corner should be carefully mitered and backed underneath by a board secured with glue and screws. Failure to do this will almost always result in a ridge (a slight shoulder) where the formica topping meets.

tween thumb and index finger. Replace the screw in the hole and seat it fully. Experience will teach how much pressure can be applied without resulting in stripping the hole. Clearance holes are needed in the backing board so that the board can be drawn snugly to the countertop. A tight clearance hole will cause a misinterpretation of the pulldown pressure required. In this case it is possible to strip the screw anchor hole and not know it. The holding power is then nil.

Basic tools for installation include drills, screwdrivers, and a level. A ratchet brace with a screwdriver bit is handy to turn the screws in the inside of a cabinet where it is difficult to make a full revolution with any other type of driver. Power drivers are quick and handy in places where a straight shot at a screw is possible.

Because of the angled approach required to set many of the cabinet hanging screws, the Phillips-head screw is preferred to the slot-head screw. Screwdriver bits do not slip out of the Phillips head as readily. Keep in mind that attachment screws should be as unobtrusive as possible. Never put a screw into a finished surface in full view.

REVIEW TOPICS

Plumbing, Heating, Electric Installing, and Insulating

1. Describe clearly the difference between a dry vent and a wet vent. Explain in your description the way Ys should face and pipes should slant.

2. Explain the options when a drain pipe needs to be run through a floor joist. *Cite* the regulations involved.

3. Explain the difference between a plenum trunk system and a box plenum and pipe system of air distribution. Also mention where each is adapted to fit best.

4. State two faults with a wall-placed heat register that will be the cause of higher heat bills.

5. Explain the effects of placing electric ceiling fixtures at third points of a long room as compared to placing them on quarter points. Recommend the better system.

6. Describe the differences and similarities of a structural cabinet soffit and a boxed-type soffit.

7. Describe the term "layering" of insulation and explain how it is done above a ceiling.

8. Describe a good way to insulate above an attic access opening in a ceiling.

Drywalling

9. List as many objectives for wallboard installing as you can remember.

10. Explain the reason for the sequence of installing the ceiling sheets first, followed by the top wall course, and last the bottom wall course.

11. Give two reasons for cutting wallboard a little shorter than the opening it will cover.

12. Describe the difference between cutting wood to fit a particular place compared to cutting gypsum board to fit an area that will be taped and finished.

13. Describe a half-height T brace, including dimensions and quantity needed to secure a wallboard in place.

14. Describe the methods of locating and providing openings in drywall panels for electric boxes.

15. Explain how to hang drywall behind cabinets where no joint is wanted between the upper and lower cabinet units.

16. Describe precisely how to position the drywall sheets in a bathroom around a tub or shower enclosure. State the type of drywall to use.

17. Explain the preferred way to install drywall over a window area and over an interior doorway area.

18. Describe the problems and usual results of attempting to fasten the ends of drywall sheets to a single ceiling joist.

19. Explain the process of attaching the ends of two sheets of drywall to a scabbed, recessed joist from start to finish.

20. Describe the correct location of gypsum board end joints to be made on a partition, including both sides of the wall.

21. Describe the technique of joining two wallboard ends between two studs and providing a cup for the tape and compound.

22. Drywall gypsum board is cut a little smaller than the area to be covered. Paneling is cut the same or slightly larger. Explain the rationale for this difference in techniques.

Molding

23. Explain the reason for butting the first molding strip to an internal corner and coping the piece that adjoins it.

Underlayment and Finish Flooring

24. Describe how to put down underlayment felt to counteract infiltration.

25. Explain all the factors involved in choosing the location of the first piece of underlayment board that will be installed.

26. Describe the two major elements in the technique of positioning the sheets of particle board so that all edges and ends touch tightly against each other.

27. Explain the technique of installing *(a)* the first piece of hardwood strip flooring, *(b)* the rest of the pieces throughout the field, and *(c)* the last course against the far wall. Cover all subjects such as positioning, nailing, cutting, and so on.

28. Describe parquet flooring and describe how to position and install it.

Installing Door Jambs

29. Explain fully how to plumb and level a door casing.

30. Write a short discourse about the two philosophies in regard to the latch edge of a wood door.

31. Explain how the bottom of a jamb may be installed to provide more efficient carpet installation and maintenance.

32. Describe how to install a door stop so that there is no bind after finish is applied. Include a method of removing and adjusting the door stop for more clearance without damage to either the jamb or the stop.

Hanging Wall Cabinets

33. Describe more than one method of locating all unseen studs in a wall on which a cabinet is to be hung.

34. Describe how to support an upper cabinet during installation with minimum help available.

35. Explain how to make a perfect miter joint at the corner of a preformed countertop.

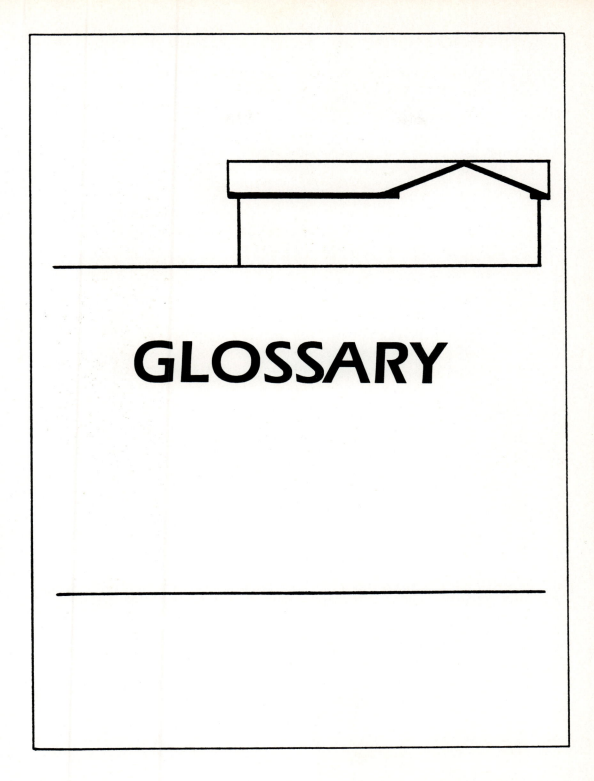

GLOSSARY

Actual size: Finished (dressed) size of lumber or real size of masonry unit.

Attic access (Scuttle):   A passageway opening through a ceiling into the attic.

Attic ventilators: Screened openings provided to ventilate an attic space.

Base or baseboard: A trim board on the bottom face of a wall around a room next to the floor.

Base shoe: Molding used next to the floor on interior baseboard. Sometimes called carpet strip.

Batten: Narrow strips of wood used to cover joints or as decorative vertical members over plywood or wide boards.

Bed molding: A molding in an angle, as between the overhanging cornice, or eaves, of a building and the sidewalls.

Bevel: An angled edge or end from one surface to the opposite surface.

Blind nailing: Nailing in such a way that the nailheads are not visible on the face of the work, usually at the tongue of matched boards.

Bonded: Attached with masonry mortar or cement.

Bowed board: The flat side of a board that curves lengthwise.

Brick ledge: A masonry bearing surface to accommodate brick. Part of a foundation wall.

Brick tie: A small, galvanized, corrugated (or rippled) strip of metal to tie hollow-core masonry walls together and to tie veneer brick to frame walls.

Brick veneer: A facing of brick laid adjacent to sheathing of a frame wall.

Building paper: Asphalt- or resin-saturated paper (felt) used for floor, siding, and shingle underlayment to block moisture and infiltration.

Butt joint: The junction where the ends of two boards or other members meet in a square-cut joint.

C

Cabinet soffits: A boxed-in framework above upper cabinets.

Call out: A short notation with an arrow leader pointing to a detail on a drawing.

Casement frames and sash: Frames of wood or metal enclosing a sash, which may be opened by means of hinges affixed to the vertical edges.

Casement window: A window hinged at the side.

Casing: Molding of various widths and thicknesses used to trim door and window openings at the jambs.

Ceiling backer: A board nailed to the top of an upper plate that overhangs the edges to provide a surface to which ceiling material is nailed.

Chords: The ceiling joists and rafter members of a roof truss.

Clamp: A device for holding objects tightly together.

Combination doors or windows: Self-storing or removable glass and screen in a seasonally convertible, exterior, protective door.

Condensation: In a building, beads or drops of water (and frequently frost in extremely cold weather) that accumulate on the inside of the exterior covering of a building when warm, moisture-laden air from the interior reaches a point where the temperature no longer permits the air to sustain the moisture it holds.

Construction, frame: A type of construction in which the structural parts are wood or depend on a wood frame for support.

Coped joint: A cut on the end of a piece of molding that mates it to the face contour of a piece it butts perpendicularly at an internal corner. *See Scribing.*

Corbel out: To build out one or more courses of brick or stone from the face of a wall to form a support for timbers. A chimney may be corbeled to change its vertical direction.

Corner bead: A strip of formed sheet metal placed on external corners of gypsum drywall or plaster lath before plastering to reinforce them.

Corner blocks: Blocks of 2 × 4s nailed to the lower ends of a corner post in a frame wall to provide a nail backing for baseboard.

Corner boards: Used as trim for the external corners of a house or other frame structure against which the ends of the siding are finished.

Cornice: Overhang of a pitched roof at the eave line, usually consisting of a facia board, a soffit for a closed cornice, and appropriate moldings.

Cornice return: The portion of the cornice that returns on the gable end of a roof overhang.

Corridor kitchen: A kitchen with parallel cabinets on opposite walls with a traffic pattern running through.

Course: Any single layer or row of material units (bricks, blocks, shingles, etc.).

Cove molding: A molding with a curved concave face used as trim to finish interior corners.

Crooked board: A board curved lengthwise on its edge.

Crown molding: A molding used on a cornice or wherever an internal horizontal corner is to be covered (between the wall top and the ceiling).

Cupped board: A warped board that is curved across its width.

Dado: A rectangular groove across the width of a board or plank.

Dead load: The weight of materials that are nonmovable (static) after construction.

Decay: Disintegration of wood or other substance through the action of fungi.

Deck sheating: Sheating on floor or roof. *See also* Sheathing.

Dimension: *See* Lumber, dimension.

Dimension lines: A narrow line with figures telling the size of something or distance between two points.

Direct nailing: To nail perpendicular to the initial surface or to the junction of the pieces joined. Also termed *face nailing*.

Distribution panel: An auxiliary breaker or fuse box at a distance from the main service entrance.

Door header: A lintel above a door to channel the bearing weight of the roof onto the trimmer studs.

Door jamb, interior: The surrounding case into which and out of which a door closes and opens. It consists of two upright pieces, called side jambs, and a horizontal head jamb.

Double-hung window: A window where the top and bottom sections move up and down.

Double plate: Two-piece, upper horizontal member of a frame wall, tying partitions and walls together.

Double wired: Attaching lapped ends of rerods together in two places with wire.

Downspout: A pipe, usually of sheet metal, for carrying rainwater from roof gutters to a suitable drain.

Drain tile: Underground piping used to carry off unwanted water. Synthetic or vitreous clay material.

Dressed and matched (Tongued and grooved):   Boards or planks machined in such a manner that there is a groove on one edge and a corresponding tongue on the other.

Dressed lumber: Lumber that has been planed.

Dry rot: A fungus disease of wood derived from dampness causing the wood fibers to disintegrate into powder.

Drywall: Interior covering material, such as gypsum board, that is applied in large sheets.

Ducts: In a house, usually round or rectangular metal pipes for distributing warm or cool air.

Duplex outlet: An electrical outlet with two openings for plugs.

El kitchen: A kitchen with counters at right angles around one corner. L-shaped cabinetry.

Facia (or fascia): A flat board, band, or face, used sometimes by itself but usually in combination with moldings, located at the outer face of the cornice.

Fall: The amount of slant (or slope) per foot of a drainpipe or surface.

Filler, wood: A heavily pigmented preparation used for filling and leveling off the pores in open-pored woods.

Fixture, electric: A lighting device to hold a light bulb.

Flanker window: Venting-type window alongside of another picture window (by a door, they are nonventing).

Frame wall: A structural wall made of studs, plates, and sheathing.

Framing, balloon: A system of framing a building in which all vertical structural elements of the bearing walls and partitions consist of single pieces extending from the top of the foundation sill plate to the roof plate and to which all floor joists are fastened.

Framing, platform: A system of framing a building in which floor joists of each story rest on the top plate of the story below or on the foundation wall of the first story.

Frieze: In house construction, a horizontal trim piece between the top of the siding and the soffit of the cornice.

Fungi, wood: Microscopic plants that live in damp wood and cause mold, stain, and decay.

Furring: Strips of wood or metal applied to a wall or other surface to serve as a fastening base for finish material.

G

Gable: The sided portion of the roof above the eave line at the ends of a double-sloped roof.

Gable end: An end wall having a gable.

Gable vent: A triangular or rectangular ventilating area high in the end of a gable wall.

Grain: The direction, size, arrangement, appearance, or quality of the fibers in wood.

Grain, edge (vertical): Edge-grain lumber has been sawed parallel to the pith of the log and approximately at right angles to the growth rings (i.e., the rings form an angle of 45° to 90° or more with the face of the piece).

Grain, flat: Flat-grain lumber has been sawed parallel to the pith of the log and approximately tangent to the growth rings (i.e., the rings form an angle of less than 45° with the surface of the piece).

Grain, quarter sawn: Another term for edge grain.

Grounds: Guides used around openings and at the floorline to strike off wet plaster; narrow strips of wood or wide subjams.

Gutter or eave trough: A shallow channel or conduit of metal or wood set below and along the eaves of a house to catch and carry off rainwater from the roof.

Gypsum board: A sheet form of plaster covered with paper ready to be installed on walls and ceilings.

H

Habitable structure: A building that will be lived in by people.

Hardware cloth: ¼ or ½″ galvanized mesh.

Header: A beam placed perpendicular to joists and to which joists are nailed in framing around a chimney, stairway, or other openings.

Header band: A dimension board nailed perpendicularly across the ends of floor joists.

Header trimmer: A shortened stud that supports the ends of a header.

Hollow-core door: A door made with two plywood faces and a core filled with stiffeners.

Hopper window: A single-section window, hinged at the bottom, that opens in.

I

Impregnated: Injected or saturated throughout.

INR (Impact noise rating): A single-figure rating that provides an estimate of the impact sound-insulating performances of a floor/ceiling assembly.

Insulation blanket: Fiberglass insulation packaged in continuous rolls or precut stud-length pieces, unfaced or backed with a vapor barrier.

Insulation board, rigid: A structural building board made of coarse wood or cane fiber in ½ and $^{25}/_{32}"$ thicknesses. It can be obtained in various-sized sheets, in various densities, and with several treatments. Some forms are rated high enough for corner bracing. Blackboard, fiberboard, insulboard.

Insulation, thermal: Any material high in resistance to heat transmission that, when placed in the walls, ceiling, or floors of a structure, will reduce the rate of heat flow.

Interior finish: Material used to cover the interior framed areas, or materials of walls and ceilings.

J

Jamb: The side and head lining of a doorway, window, or other opening.

Joint: A junction where two materials are joined together by a specific method.

Jointer: An adjustable table machine to plane smooth one edge or surface of a board at a time.

$$\boxed{\text{K}}$$

K brace: A double-angled corner brace in a wall frame.

$$\boxed{\text{L}}$$

Lap joint: Two boards that run past each other and are nailed together.

Light: Space in a window sash for a single pane of glass; also, a pane of glass.

Lintel: A horizontal structural member that supports the load over an opening such as a door or window; masonry lintel.

Live load: Loads that are occasional or movable; not built in.

Louver: An opening with a series of horizontal slats so arranged as to permit ventilation but to exclude rain, sunlight, or vision. *See also* Attic ventilators.

Lower chord: The ceiling joist member of a roof truss.

Lumber: Lumber is the product of the sawmill and planing mill not further manufactured other than by sawing, resawing, and passing lengthwise through a standard planing machine, cross-cutting to length, and matching.

Lumber, boards: Yard lumber less that 2″ thick and 2″ or more wide.

Lumber, dimension: Yard lumber from 2″ to, but not including, 5″ thick and 2″ or more wide. Includes joists, rafters, studs, planks, and small timbers.

Lumber, dressed size: The dimension of lumber after shrinking from green dimensions and after machining to size or pattern.

Lumber, matched: Lumber that is dressed and shaped on one edge in a grooved pattern and on the other in a tongued pattern.

Lumber module: Standardized thickness, width, and length, as applied to spacing.

Lumber, yard: Lumber of those grades, sizes, and patterns that are generally intended for ordinary construction, such as framework and rough coverage of houses.

M

Match lumber: *See* Lumber, matched.

Millwork: Generally, all building materials made of finished wood and manufactured in millwork plants and planing mills are included under the term millwork. It includes such items as inside and outside doors, window and door frames, blinds, porchwork, mantels, panelwork, stairways, moldings, and interior trim. It normally does not include flooring, ceiling, or siding.

Miter joint: The joint of two pieces at an angle that bisects the corner. For example, the miter joint as the side and head casing of a door opening is made at a 45° angle.

Modular design: A working plan conceived to accept standardized units of material without custom fitting and excessive waste.

Modular material: A material fabricated to a coordinated size. Typical units such as a $4' \times 8'$ plywood sheet and an $8'' \times 8'' \times 16''$ concrete block.

Module: A selected unit of measure.

Module tub or shower: A synthetic (fiberglass) one-piece unit (combination tub and shower or shower alone).

Modulus: A small unit; a divisible part of a larger module.

Moisture content of wood: Weight of the water contained in the wood, usually expressed as a percentage of the weight of the oven-dry wood.

Molding: A wood strip having a curved or projecting surface used for decorative purposes.

Mortice: A slot cut into a board, plank, or timber to receive the tenon of another board, plank, or timber to form a locking joint.

Mullion: A vertical bar or divider in the frame between windows, doors, or other openings.

Muntin: A small member that divides the glass or openings of sash or doors.

Nail pattern: A specific or designated place to put nails in a board; an organized spacing pattern.

Newel: A post to which the end of a stair railing or balustrade is fastened. Also, any decoratively turned post.

Nominal: The specified size of a building product or material. Lumber size before dressing.

Nonbearing partition: A dividing wall that carries only its own material weight. Does not support ceiling or roof components.

Nonstructural: Materials or position not intended to support additional loads other than its own weight (such as a nonbearing partition).

OA (Overall): Overall means the largest dimension of height, width, or length.

OC (On-center): The measurement of spacing for studs, rafters, joists, and the like, in a building from the center of one member to the center of the next.

OG (or Ogee): A molding with a profile in the form of a letter S; having the outline of a reversed curve. OG rain gutter.

![P]

P trap: A P-shaped piece of drain equipment used to stop fumes from backing up into a room.

Panel: In house construction, a thin flat piece of wood, plywood, or similar material framed by stiles and rails as in a door or fitted into grooves of thicker material, with molded edges for decorative wall treatment.

Paneling: A thin wall covering of wood or fabricated synthetics; usually, 4′ × 8′ sheet size.

Paper, building: A general term for papers, felts, and similar sheet materials used in buildings without reference to their properties or uses.

Paper, sheathing: A building material, generally paper or felt, used in wall and roof construction as a protection against the passage of air and sometimes moisture.

Partition: A wall that subdivides spaces within any story of a building.

Penny: As applied to nails, it originally indicated the price per hundred. The term now serves as a measure of nail length and is abbreviated by the letter d.

Perlite: A pour/fill-type insulation made from obsidian or other vitreous rock. Looks like glass pellets.

Plaster grounds: *See* Grounds.

Plenum: The main heat-distribution box of a furnace duct system.

Plumb: Vertical.

Plumbing access: A wall opening behind rough plumbing for inspection and repair purposes.

Ply: A term to denote the number or layers of veneer in plywood or layers in built-up materials in any finished piece of such material.

Plywood: A sheet of wood made of three or more layers of thin wood joined with glue. Usually laid with the grain of adjoining plies at right angles. Most plywood has an odd number of plies to create stiffness and a nonsplitting character.

Pores: Wood cells of comparatively large diameter that have open ends and are set one above the other to form continuous tubes. The openings of the vessels on the surface of a piece of wood are referred to as pores or grain.

Preservative: Any substance that for a reasonable length of time will prevent the action of wood-destroying fungi, borers of various kinds, and similar destructive agents when the wood has been properly coated or impregnated with it.

Primer: The first coat of paint in a paint job that consists of two or more coats; also, the paint used for such a first coat.

Putty: A type of filler usually made of whiting and boiled linseed oil, beaten or kneaded to the consistency of dough, and used in sealing glass in sash, filling small holes and crevices in wood, and for similar purposes.

Quarter-round: A small molding that has the cross-section shape of a quarter-circle.

R

Rabbet: A rectangular, longitudinal ell cut out of the edge of a board or plank; shiplap.

Radial saw: An overtable, cutting, circular power saw that runs on a track. There are two axis adjustments, which facilitate cutting simple and compound miters in addition to basic perpendicular crosscutting and ripping. Basically, a cutoff saw.

Recessed entrance: An entrance back from the regular wall line or one lower than floor level.

Recessed floor: A floor constructed at a lower level than the other floors. Sunken living room.

Reflective insulation: Sheet material with one or both surfaces of comparatively low heat emissivity, such as aluminum foil.

Relative humidity: The amount of water vapor in the atmosphere, expressed as a percentage of the maximum quantity that could be present at a given temperature.

Ribbon (Girt): Normally, a 1 × 4 or 1 × 6 board let into the studs horizontally to support ceiling or second-floor joists.

Rough sill: A single- or double-frame member placed horizontally below a window opening.

S

S4S: A board surfaced on all four surfaces.

Sash: A single window light frame containing one or more lights of glass. The opening part of a window casement.

Saturated felt: A felt that is completely impregnated with tar or asphalt.

Scratch coat: The coat of plaster that is scratched to form a bond for the next coat.

Screed: A small strip of wood, usually the thickness of the plaster coat, used as a guide for plastering. A straight edge for leveling concrete over forms.

Scribing: (a) Fitting woodwork to an irregular surface. In moldings, cutting the end of one piece to fit the molded face of the other at an interior angle instead of mitering. (b) Marking with a sharp instrument.

Sealer: A finishing material, in paste or liquid form, either clear or pigmented, that is usually applied directly over uncoated wood for the purpose of sealing the surface.

Service panel: The main electrical entrance box into the house containing breakers or fuses.

Shake: A thick, handsplit shingle, resawed to form two shakes.

Sheathing: The structural covering, usually wood boards, waferboard, or plywood, used over joists, studs, or rafters of a structure; also called sheeting.

Sheathing paper: *See* Paper, sheathing.

Shim: A thin piece of material used to separate or hold up parts.

Siding: The finish covering of the outside wall of a frame building. Made of horizontal weatherboards, vertical boards with battens, shingles, or other materials (aluminum, steel, vinyl, brick veneer, and stone).

Siding, bevel (Lap siding):   Wedge-shaped boards used as horizontal siding in a lapped pattern.

Siding, Dolly Varden: Beveled wood siding that is rabbeted on the bottom edge.

Siding, drop: Usually ¾″ thick and 6″ and 8″ wide with tongue-and-groove or shiplap edges. Often used without sheathing in secondary buildings.

Soffit: Usually, the underside of an overhanging cornice; also, kitchen cabinet soffit.

Soffit vent: Single, multiple, or continuous venting under the eave that directs an upflow of air over the top plate into the attic.

Specs: A shortened spelling of the word "specifications."

Splash block: A small, grooved masonry block on the ground surface to carry away rainwater from downspouts.

Split-wired outlet: A duplex with one outlet live and the other switched.

Square: A unit of measure, 100 square feet. Usually associated with roofing material.

Stack: A plumbing vent pipe that exits through the roof.

Staggered nails: Nails not placed in the same grain line nor in a straight line.

Staggered sheathing: A pattern of layment where the butt joints of adjacent courses of sheathing do not end on the same joist or rafter.

Standpipe: A vertical drainpipe for an automatic washing machine.

Stile: An upright framing member in a panel door.

Stool: An interior flat molding fitted on top of the sloping surface of the windowsill jamb. Forms a weather seal for the sash.

Storm sash or storm window: An extra window usually placed on the outside of an existing one as additional protection against cold weather.

Stringline: A tightly drawn string with which to judge straightness of building components.

Strip flooring: Wood flooring consisting of narrow, matched strips (tongue and groove).

Stud: One of a series of slender wood or metal vertical structural members placed as supporting elements in walls and partitions. Plural: Studs or studding.

Subfloor: Boards or plywood laid on joists over which a finish floor is to be laid. A work surface during construction.

Suspended ceiling: A ceiling system supported by hanging it from the overhead structural framing.

$$\boxed{\text{T}}$$

Tee: A pipe or tile component that connects lines that meet at right angles. Shaped like a T.

Three-way switch: One of a pair of switches that controls a light from two locations.

Threshold: A strip of wood or metal with beveled edges used over the finish floor and the sill of exterior doors.

Toenailing: To drive a nail at a slant with the initial surface in order to hold it to another board at right angles (more or less).

Tongue and groove: *See* Dressed and matched.

Tract-built house: One of a group of houses built on a site, usually by the same contractor.

Trim: The finish materials in or on a building, such as moldings, applied around openings (window trim, door trim) or at the floor and ceiling of rooms (baseboard, cornice, and other moldings).

U kitchen: A kitchen with counters and appliances arranged in the shape of a rectangular U. No through traffic.

Undercoat: A coating applied prior to the finishing or top coats of a paint job. It may be the first of two or the second of three coats. Prime coat.

Underlayment: A material placed under finish coverings, such as flooring or shingles, to provide a smooth, even surface for applying the finish.

Uniform single header: A one-piece 2 × 10 header approximately centered over a horizontal trimmer. Used throughout the interior partitions.

Vapor barrier: Material used to retard the movement of water vapor through walls or floors and prevent condensation in living quarters. Applied separately over the warm side of exposed walls or as a part of the batt or blanket insulation. Plastic under concrete slab floors.

Veneer: Thin sheets of wood made by rotary cutting or slicing of a log.

Vent stack: A plumbing vent pipe that exits through the roof.

Vermiculite: A mineral closely related to mica, with the faculty of expanding on heating to form lightweight material with insulation quality. Used as bulk insulation and also as aggregate in insulating and acoustical plaster and in insulating concrete floors.

Wall backers: Wood backing boards placed behind areas in the wall where things will be fastened (towel racks, curtain rods, etc.). Provides solid screw anchorage.

INDEX